UNLOCKING

SUCCESS

Published by SuccessBooks®, Lake Mary, FL.

SuccessBooks® is a registered trademark.

ISBN: 979-8-9918645-0-3
LCCN: 2024922777

This publication is designed to provide accurate and authoritative information with regard to the subject matter covered. It is sold with the understanding that the publisher is not engaged in rendering legal, accounting, or other professional advice. If legal advice or other expert assistance is required, the services of a competent professional should be sought. The opinions expressed by the authors in this book are not endorsed by SuccessBooks® and are the sole responsibility of the author rendering the opinion.

Scripture quotations marked ESV are from The ESV® Bible (The Holy Bible, English Standard Version®), copyright © 2001 by Crossway, a publishing ministry of Good News Publishers. Used by permission. All rights reserved.

Most SuccessBooks® titles are available at special quantity discounts for bulk purchases for sales promotions, premiums, fundraising, and educational use. Special versions or book excerpts can also be created to fit specific needs.

For more information, please write:

SuccessBooks®
3415 W. Lake Mary Blvd. #950370
Lake Mary, FL 32795
or call 1.877.261.4930

Visit us online at: www.CelebrityPressPublishing.com.

UNLOCKING

INSPIRING TALES *of* RESILIENCE,

SUCCESS

INNOVATION, *and* GROWTH

SUCCESS
BOOKS®

Lake Mary, FL

CONTENTS

CHAPTER 1

UNLOCKING THE SECRETS TO SUCCESS

BY Jack Canfield

*"Life is like a combination lock. Your job is to
find the right numbers, in the right order, so
you can have anything you want."*
—BRIAN TRACY

uccess doesn't happen by chance. It's the result of clear intentions, focused actions, and unwavering perseverance. In fact, if you've been thinking lately that your dreams seem further away than ever, the key to unlocking your own potential is to create a success plan that gives you specific goals to work toward.

Research from Harvard Business School shows that individuals who set clear goals and consistently work toward them are ten times more likely to achieve significant life outcomes. Ten times more likely!

So what are the secrets to success that you can learn and master on your way to creating the life you want?

DECIDE WHAT YOU WANT

One of the most crucial steps toward achieving any type of success—whether professional, personal, or lifestyle success—is simply *deciding what you want*. While that may sound simple, you'd be surprised how many people say, "I want more success in my life," without clearly defining what those wants are. Their efforts become scattered and unfocused, leading to frustration and stagnation. But deciding what you want actually serves as the cornerstone for all your subsequent actions and strategies.

Be clear and specific.

Deciding what you want begins with clarity. Vague desires such as "I want to be rich," or, "I want to be happy," are not enough. You need to translate these broad ambitions into specific, measurable objectives. For instance, instead of saying, "I want to be successful," clarify what success looks like for you. Is it reaching a particular position in your career? Is it achieving a specific financial milestone? Or perhaps it's launching and growing your own business. By defining your goals with precision, you set a clear target to aim for, making it easier to create actionable plans.

Decide what you want in every major area.

To determine what you truly want, take some time to think deeply about what you want in the major areas of life. What are your passions, interests, and core values? What activities invigorate you? What are you naturally drawn to? Understanding your true desires and motivators will help you set goals that represent your authentic self, instead of goals that are influenced by external pressures or what society expects of you.

Set aside some quiet time to do the following exercise, writing down your wishes as you think through what you truly want in the seven major areas of life.

Financial: Write down your specific financial goals. How much do you want to earn annually? By when do you want to achieve these income levels?

Career: Outline your career aspirations. What positions do you want to hold? What milestones do you want to reach, and by when?

Recreation: List the hobbies and leisure activities you want to pursue. How often do you want to engage in these activities, and by when?

Health and fitness: Specify your health and fitness goals. What weight, fitness level, or lifestyle habits do you aim to achieve, and by when?

Relationships: Describe your ideal relationships. What qualities do you seek in your personal and professional relationships? By when do you want to strengthen or build these connections?

Personal development: Identify the skills or knowledge you want to acquire. What courses or experiences do you plan to undertake, and by when?

Community and contribution: Define your goals for community involvement. What causes do you want to support, and how do you want to contribute, and by when?

By going through this exercise and writing down your specific and measurable goals in each area, you'll create a comprehensive blueprint for an exceptional future. Not only will this kind of clarity keep you motivated; it will also give you the ultimate road map for achieving your desires.

BELIEVE IT'S POSSIBLE

What's the next step in unlocking your compelling future? Instilling in your mind the *transformative power of belief*—specifically, the belief that achieving your goals is possible (not only for others but for *you* too).

When you truly believe that your goals are within reach, you trigger a series of psychological and physiological responses that align your actions with your aspirations. This alignment is essential because the journey to success is often filled with challenges and setbacks. Without a deep-seated belief in the possibility of success, these obstacles can seem insurmountable. With a strong belief, however, these same obstacles become manageable, and even motivating, as they are seen as temporary hurdles rather than permanent barriers.

Be open to possibilities and opportunities.

To believe in the possibility of success, you must first cultivate a positive and growth-oriented mindset. This involves letting go of limiting beliefs that can impede your progress. Limiting beliefs are deep-rooted notions that convince us of our inadequacies or the impossibility of our goals. They might stem from past experiences, societal conditioning, or negative self-talk.

Overcoming these requires a conscious effort to reframe your thoughts. Techniques such as affirmations, visualization, and positive self-dialogue are powerful tools in this process. By consistently reinforcing positive beliefs, you gradually shift your mindset to one that is open to possibilities and opportunities.

Experience the power of visualization.

By vividly imagining your goals as already achieved, you create a mental blueprint that causes you to take the actions, think the thoughts, and make the connections in your daily life that will bring about your goals. Visualization actually engages and empowers your subconscious mind, which cannot distinguish between experiences that are real and just vividly imagined.

Imagine how much your belief in yourself will soar once you "practice" achieving your goals during the visualization process. Not only will the newfound conviction in your subconscious mind strengthen your belief that your goals are within reach, but it will also prepare your mind and body to act as if those goals are already achieved. The more detailed and emotionally charged your visualizations, the more powerful this belief becomes, instilling a sense of certainty and inevitability about your success.

Use affirmations.

Affirmations are another tool to cement your belief in what's possible. These are positive statements that you repeat to yourself regularly, reinforcing your goals and capabilities. For instance, affirmations like, "I am capable of achieving my goals," or, "I am constantly grateful, as success comes naturally to me," help to counteract negative self-talk and build a resilient mindset. Repeating your personally written affirmations embeds them in your subconscious, gradually improving your self-image and boosting your confidence.

Surround yourself with positive people.

The environment you immerse yourself in plays a significant role in shaping your beliefs. Surrounding yourself with positive, supportive people who believe in you and your goals can amplify your own belief in what's possible. These people can provide encouragement, constructive feedback, and inspiration, helping you maintain your belief even during challenging times.

CHUNK IT DOWN

Another key to unlocking success is to tackle big goals by breaking them down into small, manageable, actionable steps—making even the most daunting goals seem less overwhelming and more attainable. When you "chunk it down," each step becomes manageable—something you can focus on individually—turning a seemingly impossible feat into a series of achievable milestones.

Use mind mapping to chunk it down.

Mind mapping is an effective technique for determining these smaller steps. It's a visual tool that helps you organize and break down complex ideas into simpler, interconnected elements. It allows you to see the relationships between various components of your goal, providing clarity and direction.

To create a mind map, follow these steps:

Start with the central idea. Begin by writing your main goal in the center of a blank page. Draw a large circle around this goal. This central idea becomes the core, or hub, of what you want to achieve.

Add major categories. Surround the central idea with branches representing major categories, or components, of the goal. For instance, if your goal is to launch a new business, your main branches might include "Market Research," "Business Plan," "Funding," and "Marketing Strategy."

Expand with sub-tasks. From each major category, draw additional branches for sub-tasks, or smaller steps, required to accomplish each category. Under "Market Research," you might add branches for "Industry Analysis," "Competitor Research," and "Customer Surveys."

Further break down. Continue to break down each sub-task into even smaller actions needed to accomplish the tasks. For example, under "Customer Surveys," you could list tasks such as "Design Survey," "Distribute Survey," and "Analyze Results."

Review and prioritize. Once your mind map is complete, review it to ensure that all necessary components are included. Prioritize the tasks based on their importance and sequence. This will help you create a clear action plan and timeline.

By mind mapping any goal (or using a spreadsheet to list tasks), you can transform a large, intimidating project into a structured plan with clear, actionable steps. Not only does this method make the process more manageable; it also helps you maintain focus and motivation. Plus, each completed "chunk" gives you a sense of accomplishment, keeping you energized, motivated, and on track.

TAKE ACTION

Of all the habits and behaviors I write about in my book *The Success Principles™*, taking action on your goals is the one tactic that will move you—further and faster—from where you are now to where you want to be. Action is the bridge between planning and results. Without action even the most well-thought-out goals remain only dreams.

Practice The Rule of 5.

When *Chicken Soup for the Soul®* was first published, our goal was to create a *New York Times* number one best seller. With that goal in mind, we interviewed dozens of book-marketing experts and sought the advice of numerous bestp-selling authors. After receiving literally hundreds of strategies, we could pursue, to be honest, our goals got a little overwhelming. Then one day we were talking to a friend who reminded us that even the largest tree could be felled simply by swinging an ax at its trunk just five times a day. "Eventually," he concluded, "the tree will have to come down, no matter how large."

Out of that advice, we developed The Rule of 5: accomplishing five simple things every day that will move you closer to completing your goal.

In the case of *Chicken Soup for the Soul*, it meant doing five radio interviews a day. Or sending out five review copies to newspapers every day. Or asking five pastors to use a story from the book in their sermons. Or calling five companies to buy a copy for all their workers. Or sending five press releases a day. And on and on, every day for more than two years. And *Chicken Soup for the Soul* did reach number one on the New York Times best-seller list, and it stayed there for three years!

Maintain a bias for action.

Many people have had good ideas—some of which have led to entirely new industries or never-before-seen ways of making money. Of course, the internet in its infancy was a place where many people had good ideas. But how many of those people took action and created the Googles, Amazons, Facebooks, and other businesses we know today?

The fact is, while most people know a lot about making money or getting results or creating advancement in the world, only a few actually get to enjoy the rewards of this knowledge (whether financial, professional, or otherwise)—simply because the rest don't take consistent action on their ideas.

Successful people, on the other hand, have a bias for action.

More than any other characteristic, action is what separates the successful from the unsuccessful—the people who actually reap the rewards from those who would merely like to.

Perhaps you too had a great idea at one time—only to see it turned into a successful business or new invention or popular product by someone else because they took action and you did not. The reality is that in the world today the people who are rewarded are those who take action.

We're paid for what we do.

Two different kinds of action.

As you pursue your goals, it's essential to understand the difference between *obvious actions* and *inspired actions*. Both are effective.

Obvious actions are practical steps such as acquiring specific skills, completing certifications, or creating a detailed business plan—steps that I often call "the next most obvious action." These requirements are discovered through research, coaching, and studying successful examples. They provide a clear sequence of steps toward achieving your goals.

Inspired actions, on the other hand, come from intuitive insights and gut feelings. These might manifest as sudden ideas or urges to take specific steps, such as reaching out to a former colleague or attending a conference. To cultivate inspired actions, engage in practices such as visualization, affirmations, and meditation, and always be ready to write down these insights as they arise.

KEEP YOUR EYE ON THE PRIZE

What could you accomplish if you maintained unwavering focus on your goals, even when faced with significant challenges?

In 2005, nineteen-year-old Maggie Doyne founded BlinkNow, a nonprofit dedicated to improving the lives of children in Nepal. After traveling to Nepal, Doyne was deeply moved by the plight of orphaned and impoverished children. Despite having no formal background in nonprofit management, she committed herself to creating a better future for these children. Doyne's intense focus led her to build a children's home, provide education, and support community-development projects. Her dedication and relentless efforts have transformed the lives of hundreds of children and families in Nepal. Doyne's story is a powerful testament to how focusing on a clear goal can lead to profound and lasting impact.

Strategies for sustained focus.

To effectively maintain focus on *your* goals, use the following strategies:

Visualize success. Regularly picture yourself achieving your goal. This mental practice helps keep your ultimate objective in view and reinforces your commitment. Visualization acts as a powerful motivator, making your goals feel more attainable.

Set clear milestones. Break your larger goal into smaller, actionable milestones. Each milestone represents a step forward, helping you track progress and stay motivated. Celebrating these achievements maintains your momentum and enthusiasm.

Cultivate resilience. View obstacles as opportunities for growth rather than setbacks. Embracing challenges as part of your journey strengthens your resilience. A resilient mindset ensures you continue striving toward your goals despite difficulties.

Build a support network. Surround yourself with people who support you and can encourage your vision. Their belief in you and your goals can reinforce your own commitment and provide motivation during challenging times.

———◆———

Mastering the journey to your own success requires first deciding what you want, then believing that what you want is possible. By breaking down your goals into manageable steps, taking decisive action, and maintaining unwavering focus, you too can transform your professional, personal, and lifestyle goals into dramatic achievements.

About Jack

Known as America's number one success coach, Jack Canfield is the founder and chairman of The Canfield Training Group in Santa Barbara, California, which trains and coaches entrepreneurs, corporate leaders, managers, sales professionals, educators, and the general public in how to accelerate the achievement of their personal, professional, and financial goals.

Jack is best known as the coauthor of the number one *New York Times* best-selling Chicken Soup for the Soul® book series, which has sold more than six hundred million books in forty-nine languages, including forty-one *New York Times* best sellers.

As the CEO of Chicken Soup for the Soul Enterprises, he helped grow the Chicken Soup for the Soul® brand into a virtual empire of books, children's books, audios, videos, CDs, classroom materials, a syndicated column, and a television show, as well as a vigorous program of licensed products that includes everything from clothing and board games to nutraceuticals and a successful line of Chicken Soup for the Pet Lover's Soul® cat and dog foods.

His other books include *The Success Principles™: How to Get from Where You Are to Where You Want to Be* (now available in its 10th Anniversary Edition); *The Success Principles™ Workbook*; *The Success Principles for Teens*; *The Aladdin Factor*; *Dare to Win*; *Heart at Work*; *The Power of Focus: How to Hit Your Business, Personal and Financial Targets with Confidence and Certainty*; *You've Got to Read This Book!*; *Tapping into Ultimate Success*; *Jack Canfield's Key to Living the Law of Attraction*; *The 30-Day Sobriety Solution*; and his recent autobiographical novel, *The Golden Motorcycle Gang: A Story of Transformation*.

Jack is a dynamic speaker and was inducted into the National Speakers Association's Speaker Hall of Fame. He has appeared on more than one thousand radio and television shows, including *The Oprah Winfrey Show*, *The Montel Williams Show*, *Larry King Live*, *The Today Show*, *Fox and Friends*, and two different hour-long *PBS Specials* devoted exclusively to his work. Jack is also a featured teacher in twelve movies, including *The Secret*, *The Meta Secret*, *The Truth*, *The Keeper of the Keys*, *Tapping the Source*, and *The Tapping Solution*. Jack was also honored with a documentary produced about his life and teachings called *The Soul of Success: The Jack Canfield Story.*

Jack has personally helped hundreds of thousands of people on six continents become multimillionaires, business leaders, best-selling authors, leading sales professionals, successful entrepreneurs, and world-class athletes while at the same time creating balanced, fulfilling, and healthy lives.

His corporate clients have included Virgin Records, Sony Pictures, Daimler-Chrysler, Federal Express, GE, Johnson & Johnson, Microsoft, Merrill Lynch, Campbell's Soup, Re/Max, the Million Dollar Forum, the Million Dollar Roundtable, the Young Entrepreneurs' Organization, the Young Presidents' Organization, the Executive Committee, and the World Business Council.

He is the founder of the Transformational Leadership Council and a member of Evolutionary Leaders, two groups devoted to helping create a world that works for everyone.

Jack is a graduate of Harvard, earned his MEd from the University of Massachusetts, and has received three honorary doctorates in psychology and public service. He is married and has three children, two stepchildren, and two grandsons.

For more information, visit www.JackCanfield.com.

CHAPTER 2

REMEMBERING

By Kimberly Ku

There are moments in our lives when we know the weight of our decisions will define our core story, even as we struggle to remember our core *values.*

The weight of my decision was unbearable. I am a clinical oncologist, and I had my second child at the start of the pandemic shutdown, right during my relentless pursuit to become a partner at my practice. I had two years to achieve this goal, but it was becoming increasingly clear I was going to need to set boundaries. Every time I said yes to something at the office, I felt I was saying no to myself. In order to live my own core story, honor my values, and hold on to my sanity, I requested an extension on the deadline to become partner.

Coming from familial and cultural backgrounds that valued accomplishment, the amending of my original goal felt shameful. For years it was a failure I could not share. I have since read Michelle Obama's books, in which she mentions being the "first and only" in a room, and how such situations felt like navigating without any road map. I was the only woman in our clinic, so when I decided to request an extension, this was exactly how I felt. How would everyone at my practice react? Was this going to paint me as a stereotypical struggling career mom rather than who I really was, a highly educated doctor and mother who was committed to living within my boundaries and working in an understanding environment? My mind was inundated by negative self-talk and illogical looming fear. Would my request for an extension be seen as a breach of contract? Would everything I worked so hard for be sabotaged by an ugly dispute and a tarnished reputation? Despite the uncertainty, I remembered another key aspect of Michelle Obama's navigation: feeling the worth to show up whole. This means telling the truth, owning my struggles, taking accountability, being myself, and living my story without shame.

To my relief my colleagues were empathetic, not only granting the extension but also entering an astonishing period of collective reflection. I have since become partner, and with my core values, career, and family not only intact but elevated beyond any original imagination.

There is a quote that states, "Speak your truth, even if your voice shakes."

Finding the courage to use your voice and tell your core story can ignite a wave of impactful progress.

We now have non-partner tracks, and even among the partners we have a diversity of work options allowing us to attract top talent without imposing artificial deadlines. We are focused on growth and innovation, and now have several female doctors in the practice who have small children.

If you have a vision for your life, a goal you want to achieve, or a decision it's time to make, there are simple things you can remember to do to unlock your own success.

They are things not taught in medical school, and they don't show up on any college class curriculum. Yet if you learn to embody these practices, you'll find that you've become the very best version of yourself, and you'll at last understand your worth.

SET YOUR LEVELS

Life moves fast, sometimes by default rather than by design. Are we doing things we *get* to do or forcing ourselves to do things we *have* to do?

Level setting is a powerful tool that asks you to evaluate your life. First, get real about how big of a gap exists between where you are and where you're going. Next, set realistic, measurable benchmarks that move you closer to your goal without compromising your values. Hold yourself accountable to these benchmarks as well as your integrity of how you achieve your timelines.

That means do not split the difference when it comes to your worth. Remember, you are not part family person, part partner. I knew I wanted to tuck my kids in at night. I wanted to be present for them on the weekends. Once I knew that, I measured every decision and opportunity against that parameter, and the definition of *partner* if it was the right fit would simply have to integrate this boundary.

Not that long ago I had to decide between going to an office party or spending the evening with my kids. Before, this would have been an agonizing internal debate. Now with my core values set as my compass, I am no longer encumbered by a dilemma between two false options in the proverbial crossroads. The goal will always be the uneventful time at home with my family, and I'm comfortable with that, knowing I can catch up with work colleagues at another time.

Though it might sound like a mundane decision, it is actually a mindful, formative daily practice. After all, unlocking success is not a momentary parting of clouds in a majestic sky, but rather the seemingly tiny tedious decisions of everyday life.

Remembering your core story is not easy, but also it does not have to be complicated. Try it out yet be gentle with yourself. Enlist boundaries that are kind to others even if they may make them uncomfortable. Tell them your truth and trust that they have the strength to understand you. Ultimately, you will see yourself charting the course to a place that feels more whole. Regardless of the rooms you show up in and whether you are the first or only—you will be there as the most authentic version of yourself.

Act as If

Many of us have heard such terms as *imposter syndrome*, or *fake it 'til you make it*. These bits of well-intended advice may feel like platitudes or be taken as permission to act inauthentically. However, some old adages do hold bold truths, particularly the act of dressing up for the job you want, not the job you have.

When I was agonizing over the way others perceived me while I was on the traditional partner track, I felt as though I had somehow abandoned myself in one of the darkest places and times in my life. I had backed myself into a corner of doubt and fear, certain that I would appear weak and unqualified by the request for an extension. Then it hit me—if I were already a partner, how would I handle this? What would an aspirational partner of this practice say and do if a deadline wasn't going to be met? I imagined that a partner would show strong leadership, would craft a vision that supported the approach and would strategically consider the growth impact of positive change. I could speak confidently knowing I was putting the practice first and working to take care of the team and our patients. That small shift was all I needed to remember.

I didn't walk into that meeting in the role of candidate but rather in the mindset of a successful, curiosity-driven, abundant partner. I learned that it's best not to show up embodying the position you're in but rather the one you want!

Leverage the Power of Humility

I am, by nature, an assertive person. I was the kid in class whose hand shot up as soon as the teacher asked a question. Later, societal conditioning taught me to wait my turn. However, I never lost the desire to be the first to speak my mind.

This likely made me seem like a know-it-all or a show-off. In time I came to appreciate that the best leaders listen much more than they talk. They are deferential to others and show the deepest levels of empathy. This means not even thinking about how to posture one's own intelligence.

Talking about first and only, we have a formidable accountant in our C-suite at my practice. She is our financial guru and right hand to the partners and shareholders. She is intelligent, and a genuine joy to work with. However, at our group meetings, she always spoke last. By the time she had the floor, there would be only a few minutes left for her to cram in her agenda. Partners would even crack jokes about the negative minutes she had to land her point. I found it unfair and condescending, and asked her how she tolerated this treatment.

She told me that she lets everyone else go first, so that she learns what still needs to be said and what doesn't need to be said at all. She explained that not only does it give her the benefit of being armed with more information, but that the shortened time frame taught her to be a clear and concise communicator. Consider me schooled! I had gotten it all wrong. She didn't have to go last; she *got* to go last. And in doing so, spoke the most efficiently of anyone in the room!

It was a huge lesson for me that held several bits of wisdom.

You can learn to turn a perceived slight into a big benefit.

There is a time to speak up, and a time to sit back.

And ultimately how well someone listens is immeasurably more important than how much they talk.

RESPOND WITH EMPATHY

In my early career my focus with patients was on results. I assumed they would appreciate efficiency and a direct, assertive tone from their confident commanding doctor. Often, I watched the clock, robotically delivered the news, and regurgitated the action plan succumbing to physician-held suppositions of efficiency.

That all changed as I gradually realized these time directives conflicted with my core value of being an empathetic listener. This became blatantly obvious when I started studying the Black

Swan group on lessons in tactical empathy and negotiation skills—essentially being in the business of relationships. After all, my job was to deliver devastating news in the worst times of people's lives when they felt most physically sick and mentally in crisis. Their fear held them hostage.

One day I found myself in a room with a young woman with an aggressive form of breast cancer. We were close in age, and the prognosis was uncertain to say the least. I took a breath myself, labeling my own fears and doubts internally. Then I took center stage and told her probably I was going to sound harsh and that a cancer center was probably the last place she wanted to be. She might even feel I could at least have the compassion to add a little more sugar coating. By the end of our appointment, she reassured *me* that I was not at all harsh or uncompassionate. By giving this patient the room to show up resilient, accepting the cancer elephant in the room and the possibility for things to be imperfect, empathizing with her as opposed to unintentionally patronizing her fears in effort to save myself, we could exercise true humanity. These rooms are not an assembly line of patients. They are the origin story of human trust and rapport.

Many of us may find our jobs to not strictly align with the technical job description, but rather in positions that require an unspoken mastery of interpersonal communication. Holding raw conversations with patients takes an ongoing commitment to practicing the "soft skills" and a willingness to lean into uncomfortable conversations. It reminds me of the parable of the buffalo we observe in nature: Buffalo instinctively know that when there is a storm, they need to run into it. This will lessen the inevitable pain and losses to come. Seems this is no soft skill at all, to instinctively catalyze growth, innovation, and curiosity that ensues a fearsome storm.

Physicians must uphold the duty to first do no harm. If we lack empathy, we risk inadvertently hurting. People have families to care for and dreams to realize. They have histories and legacies. In any tough conversation, we embark on a journey that is difficult for both of us but that can lead to joy and depth even in the most seemingly hopeless of times. The time that we waste is not in the ticking office clock, but rather in the accidental ways we are oblivious of each other's suffering.

You don't have to be an oncologist to leverage the power of empathy. In any conversation you have, in any relationship you are in, make it about respecting the other side. You need not agree with them nor disprove them to show them you feel every human being deserves to be listened to. And the paradox is that this truth includes you. Practicing empathy is an awareness that even when your words may not be a comfort, your character can be.

If I Knew Then What I Know Now...

While I now enjoy my role as a partner, the true work has only just begun. My sights continually elevate as I aspire for executive leadership.

The difference now is that my worth is not tied to the titular achievement. If I could revisit my younger self, I'd implore her not to passively accept life as a series of targets or checkboxes, but rather as a beautiful, continuous adventure as a spiritual being having a human experience. I'd tell myself that money and accolades, while feeling temporarily rewarding, are detractors from that which we can actually take with us beyond time, space, and life—depth of our relationships with others, with ourselves, and the greater forces of nature that are bigger than us all. Invite yourself to grow and aspire in infinite abundance and curiosity. Honestly, my younger self would not have been ready to listen, though. So true is the difference between knowing the path and walking it.

Now I know, however, that true success lies in the intangible things that hold real value. Knowing what's important to you and intentionally building a life around those values is the real key to genuine fulfillment and lasting success.

I'll leave you with what may seem like a cliché quote but holds profound truth: Not everything that counts can be counted, and not everything that can be counted counts. True success lies in taking the leap of faith that comes in appreciating the intangible.

My hope is that you will join me in sharing your wondrous adventures. When you feel ready, please come find me. Together we will experience curiosity beyond imagination and unlock each other's successes. How beautiful the experience is of hearing and listening to an astonishing voice and realizing that voice is coming from you!

About Kimberly

Kimberly Ku, MD, is a community physician partner at Illinois CancerCare working out of central Illinois. She is a medical oncologist and hematologist entering mid-career, possessing broad research, administrative, and practice interests and capabilities as a true generalist physician partner, including triple board certifications in medical oncology, hematology, internal medicine, and additional certification in genomic cancer risk assessment. She has interest in and passion for future executive leadership opportunities, and currently her practice has sponsored and professionally supported her as ResearcHER ambassador for the American Cancer Society this year, a position that has greatly helped her to collaborate peacefully with local institutions among competing markets with her practice as well as break down barriers in diversity and inclusion.

Kim's career and fundamental passion comes in the form of building long-term relationships based upon shared core values and missions. Hence many of her projects manifest as multi-institutional collaborations in which individual stories are the building blocks of trust- and empathy-based bodies of work larger than the sum of the parts. She was able to integrate her practice into the international Pancreatic Cancer Early Detection Consortium for she is site Principal Investigator and her practice enrolled their first patient in July 2024.

Kim became a medical oncologist in the wake of losing a college friend to young onset colon cancer. This experience at a relatively formative age taught her that even the darkest chapters of life can yield lessons of curiosity and enterprises of empathy. Hence even beyond the medical world she has embarked on understanding greater endeavors of humanitarianism, in which she has been invited to the filming of a TV show with former FBI hostage negotiator, Chris Voss, *That's Right*, on the Success Network, in order to discuss how trust and empathy play important roles in business relationships. She continues to delve deeper in the unlocking of her potential for greater good through professional interactions with the Celebrity Branding Agency and the Black Swan Group.

Kim enjoys spending time with her family, including park runs and farm events with her three boys and her husband, in addition to visiting her parents in Michigan. She enjoys exercising to podcasts and watching horror films. Her personal dream is that she would like to learn how to manage her own farm with socially responsible energy use.

Learn more:

- Ku, MD, Kimberly—Illinois CancerCare
  https://illinoiscancercare.com/doctors/kimberly-ku-m-d/
- www.linkedin.com/in/kimberly-ku-78498220

CHAPTER 3

THE SECRET INGREDIENT TO SUCCESS

By Nick Nanton

T he room was electric with anticipation. I took my seat near the front, close enough to the stage to observe every movement and nuance of the speaker.

The music was loud and fun, and my heart thumped with every beat. Everyone stood as the speaker walked to center stage, a charismatic figure with a commanding presence and a booming voice. I looked around and noticed that the audience was hanging on his every word, their eyes fixed on him as though he held the secrets to the universe! I wondered what it's like to hold the attention of an entire room.

The crowd roared in approval at his well-timed jokes and poignant stories, and the enthusiasm was contagious. I felt a sense of unity with the people around me, and though I was getting caught up in the energy of it all, I was also paying close attention to how he skillfully guided the emotional transition like he was conducting an orchestra.

My intention was to attend this event as an observer, but as I became tempted to buy what he was selling, I knew I'd picked a great person to study and that I was witnessing one heck of an income stream! That day marked the beginning of my own career as a speaker, but it was a bumpy ride.

I had just gotten started in my professional career, and my business partner Jack had been in the seminar business for years. Having had a lot of success in live events, he encouraged me to speak from the stage. It was a world I'd only participated in as a spectator, but I knew that by speaking, I could get my message out to more people at one time. I just wasn't sure I knew how to do it well enough for it to work! I figured the best way forward was to study other speakers who were crushing it from the stage.

Once I gave it a shot, I was hooked! I made my first seven figures paying my own way to speak at conferences for free and giving out free copies of my book.

I spoke to groups of eight and groups of one thousand. I learned what speaking devices made people laugh, cry, and knock down your door to get a little bit of your time and work with you. I had a great routine going, so when I was invited to speak on a huge stage, I was excited for Jack to be in the audience and to show him how far I'd come.

I ran offstage at the end, my adrenaline still pumping, and found Jack in the hallway, expecting to receive an attaboy. What I got instead was this: "Nick," he said, "I don't know what that was, but it wasn't you."

I was floored! I had done exactly what I thought I was supposed to do and learned how to work an audience. I'd studied and learned how to take the audience on a journey and make a great offer.

"I see you've learned to *perform*," he said. "You've learned how to get laughs and attention, but the reason I love working with you is because you're *not* that guy! You're actually interested in helping people. You've taken on the characteristics of other speakers instead of getting on stage as yourself. The real Nick talks fast and paces back and forth, and that's what I love!"

I have a tremendous amount of respect for Jack, so I took his words to heart. All that time I thought I was doing what I was "supposed" to do, but what did it matter if I was just a collection of other people's mannerisms and conventions rather than an authentic version of myself?

It was a great lesson on the difference between success and significance. There are a lot of strategies you can deploy to get a result, but not all those strategies form a true connection or make a significant impact. Once I learned this, I started showing up on stage as myself, quirks and all, and a funny thing happened: My business grew exponentially, and my speaking career took off!

You see, there's a secret ingredient to making a deep and lasting impact on other people. It's readily available to anyone because money can't buy it. And if you allow it to guide your life and work, doors will open, opportunities will flow, and you'll sleep like a baby at night.

THE SECRET SAUCE OF SUCCESS

There are a lot of financially successful people out there. Spend ten minutes on social media, and you'll see loads of people bragging about their six-figure year or the hack for making money while they sleep. What's less common are the truly iconic people whose success lasts for decades, changes society, and transforms thousands of lives.

If you studied the people who have long, unrivaled success, you'll find that they have a few things in common. They consistently deliver excellence, they are polite to everyone, they keep their word, and they operate through a lens of service.

Sure, they deploy strategies and understand the principles of business, but what sets them apart is something totally intangible yet profoundly impactful: character.

Character is the secret ingredient that's not included in career courses, yet it makes the difference between a life authentically lived at our highest potential and a life that is wrought with drama, misalignment, and fractured relationships.

But to truly understand what character is, you've got to first understand what it *isn't*. It's not the same as personality. Someone's personality might be described as cheerful, yet that doesn't necessarily reflect moral principles. That guy that's great to have at parties might be a total liar in business.

Character is also not the same as reputation. Reputation is what others think about you, which can be based on opinions, gossip, or even misunderstandings. It's like a celebrity who might have a great reputation due to blockbuster movies but who behind the scenes treats the extras like dirt!

Skills or talents don't equate to character either. Someone might be a brilliant musician or athlete, but these abilities say nothing about their integrity.

Nor is character based on an outcome. Character doesn't care if you have a best-selling book or one million followers on Instagram (or whatever the hot new thing is when you read this chapter). It cares how you behaved while you achieved those things.

You see, character is about the deep-seated values that guide how we live our lives even when (perhaps especially when) no one is watching.

WHERE DOES IT COME FROM?

Have you ever met someone and had trouble reading them? Maybe the first time you met them, they were friendly, and the next time, they were cold as ice. If you're like me, you then spend hours wondering if you did something to upset them or if your original assessment of them was way off.

Moods and personalities change. Character stays consistent.

That's not to say we don't all have an occasional bad day, but our character shouldn't change with our moods or the weather.

It makes one wonder, Is character something we're born with or something we choose?

The answer is both. Our genetics can influence aspects of our character, just as some people have a more natural tendency toward empathy, but these are just starting points. As we grow, it's up to us to define who we are and how we want to move through the world.

From a young age we pick up behaviors and values from parents and the culture around us. For example, growing up in a family that values honesty and kindness makes us likely to adopt those traits. But what happens if we grow up in chaos and dishonesty? Are we doomed?

Of course not. I've met hundreds of people who grew up in the worst possible conditions and still have the highest character. Our innate qualities, the environment we grew up in, and our personal choices all smack into one another, and we use our free will to choose what stays and what goes. Through life we are constantly faced with choices that test and mold our principles, and over time how we choose defines who we are.

Imagine someone who's naturally shy (an innate trait) but learns from their parents the importance of helping others (learned behavior). When they see someone being treated unfairly, they might choose to speak up despite their shyness. This decision reinforces their character.

Think of character as a garden. The soil and climate conditions are the innate traits you're born with. The seeds and plants are the lessons and values you learn from those around you. How you tend to the garden—choosing to water, weed, and care for it—represents the conscious choices you make. With consistent effort and decisions, the garden flourishes, reflecting a strong and well-developed character, one that doesn't change with the weather.

Years ago I had the pleasure of meeting and interviewing Nido Qubein, the president of High Point University. He has since become a great friend and mentor. His accomplishments are extraordinary, but it's his character that makes him one of the most sought-after speakers in the country.

Qubein came to this country at age seventeen with fifty dollars in his pocket, worked hard, started multiple businesses, and became a huge success. When I sat down with him, he stressed the importance of knowing who you are, saying, "You can't be excellent Monday, Wednesday, and Friday and take Tuesday and Thursday off!"

I like to think of myself as a kind person.

But what happens when I'm stuck in traffic, navigating a

frustrating call, or dealing with a cranky cashier? Am I still kind? I sure try to be!

The secret is to be who you are, not just when things are perfect or when it's all going smoothly, but every day, no matter what.

It's not easy, and we all have human moments, me included, but I try to always leave a room or conversation better than when I entered it and be proud of my conduct. I exercise my character muscle by always being curious about how I can help solve someone's problem, and it inevitably ends up benefiting me as well.

When Qubein was working as a youth director at a church, he found that there weren't any great resources that offered retreat ideas or leadership tools. He realized he likely wasn't the only director hitting that wall, so he started a company that offered those things. He paid ten dollars an idea, and soon he had enough ideas to write the material. He started with just five hundred dollars and in three years had sixty-eight thousand customers in thirty-two countries!

He believed he could help, and he did. Imagine his delight when the chaplain for the United States Army ordered hundreds of his product for every army base in the world!

Your beliefs lead to your behaviors, and your behaviors lead to your results.

But what happens when results are not enough?

In that case you have to do what Chris Voss did and redefine success for yourself.

SUCCESS AS THE JOURNEY, NOT THE RESULT

Success is often perceived as the achievement of specific results—getting a high-paying job, winning a championship, or achieving fame. However, a more meaningful understanding of success focuses on how you conduct yourself on the journey rather than just the end results. Here's why: In January 2020 I met Chris Voss, former FBI negotiator, author of the best-selling book *Never Split the Difference*, and creator of the most successful master class in the world.

I thought he was cool but had *zero* interest in reading another negotiation book. It was bad enough trudging through them in law school. Then, when COVID hit, I was stuck and bored like everyone else but still wanted to be helpful and living purposefully, so I decided to start a podcast. I remembered my meeting with Chris and wanted to invite him to be a guest, but I knew that meant I would have to read his book first. I did, and it turned out to be one of my top ten favorite books of all time. Often when people think about the concept of negotiation, they think of there being a clear winner and a clear loser. What I love the most about Chris' style of negotiation is that he believes if you're taking something from someone, you're not actually winning.

The key is to have empathy and understand the other party's position, their fears, and their desires. When Chris was a hostage negotiator, he had no leverage. He had nothing to offer the other party except jail time! Yet he was successful in reaching a peaceful resolution in nearly all his negotiations.

He had to learn to negotiate without having any carrots to dangle, and he did it by resting on his strength of character, which allowed him to see the criminal as a human being. The *result* was never going to make the criminal happy, but the behavior and empathy demonstrated during the negotiation *could*.

I ended up producing a documentary on Chris' work called *Tactical Empathy*, and it's out now on Amazon and other major platforms. Chris and his story are a brilliant testament to how we can bring character to business, even in the most stressful, high-stakes negotiations.

The conditions may change. The characters and the end goal may change. What shouldn't change is who you are on the journey.

Finding Your Operating System

Character may not be something you spend a lot of time thinking about, yet it's always in play.

It's affecting how people experience you. It influences their opinion of you. In its unspoken nuances, it's making or breaking your relationships, your career, and your reputation.

Your character is like your personal operating system that's always running in the background of your life. For me it's the cornerstone of my business. My team and I are committed to demonstrating extraordinary character and to only working with people who share that value.

Think of your "always" and "nevers."

I *always* keep my word, and I *never* make a promise I can't keep. I *always* say yes when someone wants my opinion or mentoring in a way that fits in with my schedule, and I *always* share the best advice I have that I think can help them.

Those always/never statements are expressions of your character.

Ultimately, the secret ingredient to success doesn't boil down to the data or the profit-and-loss statement or the number of people who follow you on social media. True success lies in how others see you, and how you see yourself.

By living in integrity with your nonnegotiable values, you create a powerful, guiding framework that influences every aspect of your life. Embody it, refine it, and let it lead you to becoming the best, most impactful version of yourself.

About Nick

From the slums of Port-au-Prince, Haiti, with special forces raiding a sex trafficking ring and freeing children, to the Virgin Galactic Space Port in Mojave with Sir Richard Branson, twenty-two-time Emmy Award–winning Director-Producer Nick Nanton has become known for telling stories that connect. Why? Because he focuses on the most fascinating subject in the world: *people*. As an award-winning song-writer, storyteller, and best-selling author, Nick has shared his message with millions of people through his documentaries, speeches, blogs, lectures, songs, and best-selling books. Nick's book *StorySelling* hit The Wall Street Journal Best-Seller List and is available on Audible as an audio-book. Nick has directed more than sixty documentaries and a sold-out Broadway Show (garnering forty-three Emmy nominations in multiple regions and twenty-two wins), including:

- *DICKIE V* (ESPN/Disney+)
- *Rudy Ruettiger: The Walk On* (Amazon Prime)
- *The Rebound* (Netflix)
- *Operation Toussaint* (Amazon Prime)

Nick has shared the stage with, coauthored books with, and made films featuring:

- Larry King
- Kathie Lee Gifford
- Hoda Kotb
- Dick Vitale
- Kenny Chesney
- Magic Johnson
- Coach Mike Krzyzewski
- Jack Nicklaus
- Tony Robbins
- Lisa Nichols
- Peter Diamandis
- And many more

Nick specializes in bringing the element of human connection to every viewer, no matter the subject. He is currently directing and hosting the series *In Case You Didn't Know* (season 1 executive produced by Larry King), featuring legends in the worlds of business, entrepreneurship, personal development, technology, and sports.

Nick's first love has always been music. He has been writing songs for more than two decades, and his songs have been aired on radio across the United States and in Canada. He is currently ranked in the top 10 percent of songwriters in the world. His songs have been recorded by Lee Brice, Darius Rucker, RaeLynn, Joe Bryson, and many more, and have amassed more than three million streams on Spotify, Apple Music, Pandora, and SoundCloud. He received three Gold records in 2018 for his work with the global touring band A Day to Remember.

Nick has written and/or produced songs that have appeared on the following shows or in promotional commercials for:

- the Fox prime-time series *Glee*, *New Girl*, *House*, and *Hell's Kitchen*
- the MLB All-Star Game
- ABC Family's hit series *Falcon Beach*
- the CBS prime-time series *Ghost Whisperer* starring Jennifer Love Hewitt

CHAPTER 4

AGAINST ALL ODDS

*How to Forge an Unbreakable Spirit
in the Face of Adversity*

By Léonie Rosenstiel

The first thing I noticed was the blood all over the kitchen floor. My mother stood there, bleeding profusely from a cut on her hand. It was clear she had made no attempt to stop the bleeding or to pick up the phone and call for help.

I had walked into the house and found her covered in blood, a blank look on her face, seemingly unaware of the pain or mess around her.

That's when I knew it was time to get help.

My mother had been a very smart woman.

She was a linguist first, then joined the Army and oversaw a thousand-WAC censorship unit in New Guinea during World War II. When she came back to the US, she became a college professor. She was highly intelligent, which made her diagnosis even more devastating.

It started with not knowing what day of the week it was. Then she forgot how to pay the bills. Even as the symptoms got progressively worse, it was hard for us to accept that her brilliant mind was failing.

Eventually, the doctor confirmed signs of Alzheimer's.

We dealt with her forgetfulness. We dealt with it when she got lost in a restaurant, unable to find her way back to our table.

But when she accidentally cut herself and didn't seem to understand the gravity of the situation, and at the same time couldn't remember how to handle money, we had to face the facts.

She would need a guardian.

Little did I know that my attempt to find care for my mother would set in motion the most gut wrenching, infuriating challenge of my life.

You see, when it becomes clear that an adult can no longer safely care for themselves, there's a legal process that must be undertaken, even if the person seeking guardianship is a family member.

What most people don't know is that there are businesses that the court may appoint to act as guardians of incapacitated people. Their payment comes out of the assets of the person they're assigned to control. When those run out, if their charge is still alive, either they're paid by the state, or a public guardian takes over.

The unscrupulous ones will manipulate the system to get these appointments. Here's how it starts:

The court appoints a team to assess the situation—a team who has never met the patient and knows nothing about the family.

In my case the attorney representing me and my mother was in fact being paid by the other side.

At the end of the very confusing proceedings my attorney said, "You are now divorced from your mother. She has a guardian."

Guardianship was granted to a total stranger. My mother was already in her 90's and I was isolated from her for three years.

I was devastated. My mother would try to call me, and they'd take the phone from her hand. They told me she hated me and to leave her alone. The more I started telling people what was happening, the more horror stories I heard.

I received message after message of families sharing stories of deceit and isolation—children kept from seeing their aging parents; families being gaslighted and told that their loved one must be separated from them to bond with their new caregivers.

It was mind-blowing.

My mother remained under their guardianship for 9 years. When I was finally granted permission to visit her three years in, our conversations were supervised and highly censored.

They say it's for the patient's own good.

They say it's in their best interest.

They *lie.*

It's a system in which greed is pervasive and the number of people who must choose to act unethically and agree to the corruption is astounding.

No one thinks this can happen to them, and yet millions of people are currently under this sort of coercive guardianship despite the protests and pleading of their families.

But my mother wasn't the only one to have her freedom stolen from her by the very systems that are in place to protect us.

I was about to have my own rights compromised, and my own voice silenced.

Purpose in Pain

When I was young, my father worked to help people get housing in New York City. I remember him working with a family from Puerto Rico who had come to America with nothing. He asked my mother to gather some things for them. He meant to gather clothes, but my mother, realizing they had no furniture, gave them my parents' bed!

"We can get another bed," she said, never doubting her choice to sacrifice for another.

My parents were always fighting for the underdogs.

I was raised to fight injustices inflicted on other people. I never imagined I'd be a victim of court-imposed injustice myself.

The rage I felt after my mother's death was fueled by the realization that her final years were spent not in the presence of loved ones, but in relentless battle.

The pain of that realization ignited a determination to do whatever it took to prevent other families from enduring such needless suffering.

I was infuriated that while most court hearings are matters of public record, guardianship cases are shrouded in secrecy, allowing for the corruption to continue without notice from the public or the media.

With it all kept under wraps, the crooked agencies, judges and attorneys could keep their financial schemes running.

I told my story as often as I could. I informed the media. I wrote to every legislative body I could think of.

It must have been making them nervous because a judge imposed on me a totally unconstitutional gag order. I was being punished for making waves. The Supreme Court of New Mexico refused to hear my appeal.

I concluded that the corruption went all the way to the top.

I was not allowed to speak about my mother, or even about the entire subject of guardianship. If I did, I'd be thrown in jail for contempt of court.

I was silenced, but my friends were not. They continued to alert the press about my story, which was also the story of millions of families in America.

Even Sam Donaldson and a producer from *Entertainment Tonight* called for an interview. The gag order didn't even allow me to be polite and call them back; it prohibited me from contacting journalists or legislators.

I decided I would do whatever it took to get this gag order lifted and help as many families as I could avoid the fate I had lived through.

I'd share my story. I'd educate them. I'd help them navigate the purposely confusing proceedings.

I would not lie down and ignore these crimes against families.

We would fight. And we would *win*.

Faith Prevails

I've always been a very spiritual person, so when I needed an advocate and no one seemed to be willing, I turned to prayer.

It worked.

I found an attorney with whom I forged a profound spiritual connection and who was confident we could get the gag order lifted.

His peers told him not to take the case. Everyone around him warned him that it was a lost cause, but he was brave and refused to be intimidated or give up.

One day we were called to the offices of the opposing counsel for a deposition. On one side of the table were a witness, me, and my lawyer, and on the other side were three opposing lawyers, their witness, and my deceased mother's former guardian. Suddenly, a man from their office walked in, tapped one of the attorneys on the shoulder, and pointed to his computer screen. His face went white. Like an assembly line, each person tapped the next one on the shoulder and pointed to the laptop in front of them, all of them reacting in what can only be described as a mix of shock and disbelief.

The *Albuquerque Journal* had contacted all involved to inform them that they were going to file an amicus brief in support of the gag order being lifted.

Five years after my mother's death I was given back my voice.

The Secrets to an Unbreakable Spirit

Years before the experience with my mother, I was a teacher of spiritual healing. For seven years I taught others how to work with spiritual principles to heal, connect and pull themselves out of darkness.

I turned to these practices as a lifeline.

When you're faced with adversity, you can tap into spiritual tools as they are a reservoir of strength readily available to all of us. When used in tandem, they become a formula for forging an unbreakable spirit.

Meditation and Prayer

You may be thinking that meditation is not for you. Maybe you've tried it and couldn't quiet your mind or sit still, and that's OK. Reframe it to simply be a period of quiet connection with all that is. When you intentionally tune into the flow of the universe, your inner voice, and the frequency of nature, your biology changes. Your nervous system calms, your mind clears and in that space of silence, you're reminded of your connection to the entire Universe and everything in it.

It's tough to feel weak or defeated with a higher power in your corner.

No matter what we're going through, we can choose to believe that it's happening *for* us, not *to* us.

When we detach from victim mode, our minds sharpen, cleaning up our perspective so that our focus shifts from the pain we're in, to the problems we can solve.

One day I went to visit my mother and found that they had left her sitting in front of a very violent movie. When I walked in the room, my mother said to me, "You can't stay here. This place is going to explode!"

Of course she was confused, thinking that what she was seeing on TV was real. The attending caregiver, however, heard only one part of the conversation. "You can't stay here."

She told the guardian that my mother didn't want me there.

At that point, I had prayed and meditated and knew how to keep myself calm in the face of massive manipulation.

I recognized that this was a pattern. I began to piece together other patterns of behavior at the agency so I could work to figure out their playbook.

No matter what you're facing, cultivate a routine that connects you to a Higher Power and stay calm. Shift your focus to figuring out the patterns and to beating the challenge by overcoming it on your terms, not those of your opponent. If you can do that, you step out of a victim identity and start embodying the energy of a warrior—one who rises from the ashes, outsmarts the enemy and ultimately paves a path to victory.

BE OF SERVICE

Being in service to others is a sacred practice that helps us transcend our own personal struggles. In service, we can assign purpose and meaning to what feels like a hopeless situation.

The court had tied my hands when it came my mother, but I could guide others to avoid the same fate and doing so became a channel through which grace and healing began to flow.

I was reminded of my interconnectedness; reminded that everyone I encountered was living a story as deep and dynamic as my own; reminded that we can all be uplifted when we pool our strength, draw from the well of compassion and work together to foster peace and justice.

Today I am the founder of Dayspring Resources, an organization that exists to help families solve the complex problems associated with aging and avoid many of the pitfalls of the current system.

Most people have no idea that their own rights to freedom of speech and association might be in jeopardy.

But that's exactly what happened to me. It took me years of expensive litigation—after my mother died—to free myself from those restrictions.

Every year, over 3.5 million people turn sixty-five. This is the fastest-growing group in the United States.

Nearly half of those turning sixty-five will eventually suffer from some form of dementia and if that happens, you and your loved one could be manipulated by unscrupulous people who have an alphabet soup of degrees behind their names.

That's why I made a vow to help as many people as I could and promised my mother that I would put our story into a book. That's what I did. It's called *Protecting Mama: Surviving the Legal Guardianship Swamp* (Calumet Editions). It's a casebook showing exactly how various people manipulated us, and how I began to develop counterstrategies.

Some people have gone bankrupt trying to protect family members when the law didn't allow them to win. I cannot change what happened to my mother, but I can impart my knowledge and prevent others from becoming collateral damage.

There is great strength in service, but you don't have to take up a mission or fight legislation. When you're down, the simple act of lifting another up unlocks a wellspring of strength just when you need it the most.

An Attitude of Gratitude in Unlikely Places

Over the almost nine years that my mother was under the control of a commercial guardianship firm, I was offered varying "monetary considerations" to sign a non-disparagement agreement.

These offers varied from $500,000 to $5 million. Because the money also involved a permanent loss of my freedom of speech and their right to forever monitor everything I said, I declined.

Imagine that—attempting to pay another person to sign away their freedom! It's enough to make one lose faith in humanity, or to *gain* faith in oneself.

It's tough to be grateful and to stay in faith when you've been through hell. In those moments our energy is consumed by thoughts of "why me?" and "what now?" and "how can this be happening?"

But I've learned over the years that if I am being challenged, it is because I am being *entrusted*.

In my dark moments, I am being fortified to stand as a guide for those who come after me.

So no matter what you're going through, it is not just an unfortunate fate that has befallen you but a catalyst of change, ushered in by a higher power for a purpose greater than you can yet imagine.

That is why I never give up hope.

On my toughest days, in the midst of the most vicious battles, the sun still rises over the Sandia Mountains in the most splendid way, casting a pink glow across the land, setting in motion the bird songs, and reminding me that even in darkness, in the throes of weakness and in the pain of persecution, there is still breathtaking and unmistakable proof of a life worth fighting for.

About Léonie

For more than forty years Léonie Rosenstiel has had multiple successes as a speaker, writer, teacher, editor, publisher, and opinion leader in fields as diverse as music, ministry, and keeping families together as their elders age. Her method of dealing with the issues of aging is to expose the methods of the unscrupulous. Then, she helps families protect themselves, while strengthening family ties and protecting their financial wellbeing.

She has dealt with scores of legal professionals, including both judges and attorneys, interviewed for-profit guardians, counseled and coached families whose loved ones were torn from them by a seemingly uncaring and capricious legal system. She also acts as an information source for the clients of investment/financial planners, estate planners, coaches for mid-life women entrepreneurs/executives, and succession coaches.

The Senate Special Committee on Aging invited Léonie to submit testimony to its last hearing on aging and guardianship abuses. She now offers families the Dayspring Empowerment System to help prevent the worst abuses and assist families already enmeshed in the web of this painful process to mitigate the damage.

Léonie is the president of Dayspring Resources Inc. She is also a best-selling author of the multi-award-winning *Protecting Mama: Surviving the Legal Guardianship Swamp* as well as *Legal Protection: Affordable Options for Individuals, Families, and Small Businesses.* She has edited, written, translated, or contributed to more than twenty books. Her work has been recognized by the *New York Times*, the Boston *Globe*, the *Los Angeles Times*, and the *Washington Post*. She has also been quoted in online media as diverse as GoBankingRates.com, Google.com, and Yahoo.com, in addition to being a podcast guest and sought-after panelist.

Since 1974 Léonie has served on nonprofit boards, ranging from Professional Children's School in New York City to the Association of Traditional East Asian Medicine, Health Security for New Mexicans, SouthWest Writers, and New Mexico Press Women, the last four organizations in New Mexico.

In addition to enjoying helping others live their best lives, Léonie loves getting up early enough to sip a cup of Earl Grey tea as she watches the antics of the roadrunners in her backyard and the sunrise over the magnificent Sandia Mountains a few miles east of her Albuquerque home.

Learn more:

Website: DayspringResources.com

LinkedIn: www.linkedin.com/in/leonierosenstiel

CHAPTER 5

YOUR EPIC JOURNEY

By Gary Duvall

Mount McLaughlin majestically rises into the sky in full view over the Rogue River Valley, home of the wild Rogue River and all the other mountains, streams, and lakes in Southern Oregon. The summit is covered with snow for most of the year and towers about eight thousand feet higher than the floor of the Rogue Valley. There are stunning hiking trails in the valley and the surrounding hills to enjoy a day hike, but trekking to the summit of Mount McLaughlin is an epic journey by comparison.

Climbing up a mountain requires planning, preparation, and careful execution. If you've never done it before, you would be well served by having some experienced guides to accompany you. The guides will map out the route from the bottom to the top and back down again. They will inventory your supplies and equipment and schedule the time it should take before you begin. Many important details need to be considered like the weather, terrain and potential hazards that can be encountered along as well as contingency plans should an emergency arise.

The good news is, if you've made the decision to bring a guide, they will accompany you all the way to the top!

YOUR FINANCIAL JOURNEY BECOMES EPIC

What I have learned over the years is that life, and financial planning, are very much like climbing a mountain.

As you navigate life's peaks and valleys, storms will set in. You may encounter swollen streams and fallen trees that block your path. You may twist your ankle or find yourself face to face with sneaky predators.

Those sorts of challenges are a natural byproduct of a climb toward any summit, much as obstacles and setbacks are a byproduct of reaching for your most worthy goals. The good news is that whether you're ascending a steep cliff, working to complete a project, or planning out your financial future, there is a formula for success that will carry you through: a solid mindset, a clear vision, courageous action, and the willingness to trust the support systems you build along the way.

When I founded my financial planning and wealth management company, I named it Epic Journey Financial LLC. Our mission to guide folks along their financial journey mirrors the mission of the guides who help people navigate journeys into the wilderness. My clients seek to not only survive but *thrive* in their life's journey. They prefer to avoid mistakes and perils that negatively affect their financial security. They want to reduce or eliminate the stress and anxiety that accompanies traversing changing financial circumstances, shifting economic conditions and life changes that occur in the journey called life.

Just like in climbing, there are factors in life and in financial planning that are beyond our control. There isn't much we can do about a volatile economy or temperamental market. That's exactly why it's vitally important that we take ownership of what we *can* control!

START WITH THE END IN MIND

Many folks dread working on their finances yet enjoy planning for a vacation.

We strive to create a client experience that feels less like typical financial planning and more like anticipating their arrival at an exciting and pleasurable destination. Because that is exactly the way that it should be! Our version of financial planning starts with selecting the goals and objectives that each client really wants to reach. This is like deciding where to go on an exhilarating or relaxing annual vacation and begin planning for it. Once you select the destination the fun begins!

Jack Canfield taught me to begin by creating an exciting vision for each area of your life based on your highest purpose and values. Imagine how happy you will be when you reach your exhilarating destinations in each area of your life: career/business, relationships, recreation/free time, health/fitness, financial, personal, and community/contribution. It's vitally important to think and feel now as you will feel when you've accomplished your aspirations, financial or otherwise. So have fun and enjoy the process of visualizing all areas of your life the way you want them to be.

If, however, you're still having trouble designing your own epic journey, get yourself a sherpa.

IMAGINE YOUR SHERPAS

High in the majestic Himalayas, a group of climbers makes their way up the rugged terrain, led by the experienced and resilient Sherpas. Clad in brightly colored traditional attire mixed with modern climbing gear, the Sherpas move with an effortless grace, their faces etched with determination and a deep connection to the mountains they call home.

The Sherpas, carrying heavy loads of supplies and equipment, navigate the icy slopes and treacherous paths with a strength and agility that seems almost supernatural. Their weathered hands grip ropes and ice axes with practiced precision, guiding the climbers through the thin, crisp air that bites at exposed skin.

Around them, the landscape is a stunning panorama of snow-capped peaks, deep blue glaciers, and vast expanses of white. The sunlight glistens off the ice, casting a dazzling array of colors that reflect off the Sherpas' multicolored scarves and prayer flags attached to their packs. These flags flutter in the wind, a constant reminder of the spiritual significance of their journey.

As they ascend, the Sherpas' voices carry through the thin air, offering encouragement and instructions to the climbers. Their language is melodic and rhythmic, a soothing counterpoint to the harsh environment. The climbers, relying heavily on the Sherpas' expertise and endurance, follow their lead with a mixture of awe and gratitude.

The Sherpas' faces, bronzed by the sun and wind, occasionally break into warm smiles, their eyes crinkling with kindness. Despite the immense physical strain, they exude a sense of calm and confidence, a testament to their lifelong relationship with these formidable mountains.

In the evenings, as the group sets up camp, the Sherpas continue their work, preparing meals and ensuring that everyone is safe and comfortable. The flickering light of the campfires illuminates their faces, highlighting the deep lines and strong features that speak of countless expeditions and an unwavering spirit.

Through their tireless efforts and profound knowledge of the mountains, the Sherpas embody the true essence of teamwork and resilience, guiding the expedition with unwavering dedication and an indomitable will.

A good Sherpa is highly valued as they are often able to anticipate sudden changes in conditions, to prepare for every possibility and to calmly guide their clients through the most treacherous conditions. Their presence is reassuring to the climbers, as their decision-making framework is rooted in a deep and intimate understanding of the mountain and the surrounding region.

In fact, Sherpas are often the unsung heroes of the highest peaks!

A few years ago, I was hiking with friends about 5000 feet up a mountain. I decided to take a walk on my own to the Sky Lakes, which was about a one-day hike into the wilderness. As I set off, I realized that I didn't really know where I was going. I had a map, but the map was old and faded and offered multiple routes to my destination.

The scenery was beautiful, and I stopped to take pictures along the way, enjoying the solitude and the peaceful sounds of nature. When I finally made it to Badger Lake, I found it surrounded by driftwood and tree roots. Undeterred, I walked on, and that's when my foot got caught between fallen trees.

Luckily, I was walking slowly enough that I was able to dislodge my foot and escaped without a sprained ankle, but it did get me thinking...

If I had gotten injured, what would I have done?

I was completely alone, with a limited food supply and vulnerable to the changing temperatures and the threat of nightfall. I had no cell service and even if I did, my battery would've eventually died.

Fortunately, I made it back to camp unscathed, but it was a humbling reminder that it's best to have someone by your side to help you prepare, to share supplies with and to turn to when things go south.

The same is true in financial planning. If you're going into a wilderness that you've never navigated before, you need someone with you who knows the terrain and who ideally is skilled in all the things with which you are not trained.

Les Brown wrote, "Ask for help. Not because you are weak. But because you want to remain strong."

I realized that day on the mountain that despite having years of experience in hiking and climbing, two brains would have been better than one.

On an Everest expedition, the Sherpa goes first. They scope out the scene, they prepare, they take the supplies, they set up camp and then they come back down and retrieve their clients with full confidence that they have set their clients up for a successful climb.

But you don't have to be scaling Everest to benefit from the analogy of the Sherpa. Set a goal and find an expert you can trust.

Whatever your goal is, you'll find that when you allow yourself to be guided to the top, the view is fantastic!

Here is a sneak preview of the epic financial journey we take our clients through to help them reach the destinations they are most excited about:

Step 1: Gather base camp insights.

Every successful journey starts with preparation. We sit with our clients and gather all the necessary financial information—their starting point, aspirations, and dreams. Like setting up base-camp, you've got to establish a strong foundation to build upon. Begin by clearly defining what financial success looks like for you and creating a vivid mental picture. Picture yourself in the home you want. Picture the exact number you'd like to see in your bank account. As you envision your life of abundance, pay close attention to how it feels to live in this level of security.

Step 2: Analyze the terrain.

Just as a climber studies the mountain's terrain, you've got to be self-aware about your financial landscape. We help our clients decipher patterns, assess risks, and identify opportunities. This thorough analysis helps us chart the optimal route to your financial summit.

Step 3: Propose summit-worthy solutions.

Imagine reaching a point where you can glimpse the peak from afar. In this phase, we present you with tailored strategies and solutions. These are your climbing tools—each designed to overcome challenges and lead you closer to your financial goals.

Step 4: Implement action ascents.

With a map in hand and tools ready, it's time to ascend. Now you've got to take actionable steps that move you steadily toward your summit. Just like conquering a mountain requires perseverance, so does navigating financial changes. Nothing happens without proactive steps. I'm using financial planning as an example, but it's of course true for any goal. You need a plan that includes small, manageable steps and milestones.

For instance, if your goal is to save $50,000, determine how much you need to save each month and find ways to increase your income or reduce expenses to meet that target.

Consistency is like rocket fuel. Whether you set up automatic transfers to a savings account or make a daily habit of calculating your expenses, regular and automatic habits are the key to rapid change.

It's not rocket science, but small, simple and consistent steps lead to major results.

Step 5: Monitor the summit victory.

The summit is within sight, but a climber's journey doesn't end until they're safely back at basecamp. Similarly, you want to continually monitor your progress and make adjustments as needed. Life will throw curveballs. The market will go up and down. Unforeseen pandemics will shut down the world! We cannot control what happens outside of us, but we can remain steadfastly aware and learn to go with the flow.

I've had the pleasure of working with some of the most brilliant thought leaders in the world, like Jack Canfield for instance, and one trait I notice that they all share is the ability to be flexible and resilient in the face of change and adversity.

The journey to any goal is rarely linear.

IMAGINE!

"The imagination is literally the workshop wherein are fashioned all plans created by man. The impulse, the desire, is given shape, form, and action through the aid of the imaginative faculty of the mind."

—NAPOLEON HILL
AUTHOR, *THINK AND GROW RICH*

When I was a teenager in high school, Mr. Olson, one of my teachers, stopped me in the hallway during the lunch hour and gave me an assignment. He told me to go to the library and check out the book *Think and Grow Rich* and read it. I was puzzled by this odd assignment, and the way in which he delivered it. He stood there for the longest time, rubbing his chin, like he was deep in thought before he told me what to do. I obtained the book as instructed and read it from cover to cover. My imagination was so captured by the words of the book, that when I finished the last page, I was disappointed, so I turned back to the beginning and read the whole book again. I'm still reading that same book today, even though the pages are yellow and brittle, and the cover is ripped. It works!

Since then I have surrounded myself with life's greatest teachers, coaches and mentors. Along the way I imagined helping others to think and grow rich. I envisioned starting my own company that does exactly that and operate that company as president and CEO. In my work, my purpose is to guide others on their journey to achieving their dreams, and to ensure they have all the resources and strategies they need along the way.

I might not have the genetic makeup of a Nepalese Sherpa, but I do aim to emulate their principles.

Be strong.

Be prepared.

Be of service to my family, friends and clients.

And be vigilant in my commitment to helping everyone around me reach their full potential, no matter how treacherous the terrain, and no matter how high the summit.

I know that having plenty of money is not the ultimate key to happiness and fulfillment but as Zig Ziglar pointed out, "Money isn't the most important thing. But it ranks right up there with oxygen!"

Right now we live in the most remarkable time in the entire history of civilization, with more opportunity than most people realize. What I know now is that once you have taken the time to discover your purpose in life, you can focus your attention, time, energy and money to enjoying your journey and living that purpose to the fullest. Then you can be, do and have anything you want. It's almost ironic, but as soon as you enthusiastically pursue the dreams you're most passionate about, your life's journey instantly turns epic! Enjoy the ride!

About Gary

Gary Duvall is the founder, president, and CEO of Epic Journey Financial LLC, a financial planning and wealth-management firm. His extensive team of specialists serve as expert guides to help his clients through the financial wilderness similar to how Sherpas assist mountain climbers to the summits of tall mountains. Working closely with his financial service partner, Money Concepts, he guides others along their financial journey, including investments, risk management, estate planning, and tax planning. Enjoying the process and tracking positive forward progress makes the journey epic for Gary's clients.

Before graduating from Rogue River High School, Gary had already become an avid student of success philosophy. He turned this passion into a lifetime avocation of learning how to enjoy health, wealth, and wisdom, and now helps others do the same. Gary has a reputation for making complex topics easily understood and is known for not talking over your head.

He is now entering his thirty-ninth year of marriage to his wife, Carol, who also graduated from high school locally. Their daughter Calley, who turned thirty-six this year, also lives in the beautiful Rogue River Valley, and the whole family loves the creeks, streams, and rivers that flow through the mountains and valleys of Southern Oregon.

Gary is a graduate of Southern Oregon University with a Bachelor of Science in business administration. He holds the Chartered Retirement Planning Counselor (CRPC)® designation from the College for Financial Planning®. Gary is a qualifying and life member of the Million Dollar Round Table (MDRT), The Premier Association of Financial Professionals®, with twenty-two consecutive years of membership. He is a two-time best-selling author and has been seen on ABC, CBS, NBC, and Fox TV.

Gary Duvall, CRPC®
President and CEO
Epic Journey Financial LLC
(541) 690-1096
www.epicjourneyfinancial.com
gary@epicjourneyfinancial.com

CHAPTER 6

THE UNSHAKABLE POWER OF RESILIENCE

By Buthiana Hassan

I was just four years old when my entire world unraveled. I was my father's princess. Every day after work, he would hoist me up high, making me feel special. But when he suddenly died, my family was thrown into poverty. My mother was left to care for me and my four siblings with very few resources. Defying cultural norms and refusing to live with my father's brother and his other wives, she resolved, "I am moving out, dignity above all." That was the day I understood the true meaning of resilience and the day my story begins. She moved us into a run-down shantytown, in Sudan, where I learned that knowing and trusting oneself and harnessing inner strength is the path to a purposeful life and true success. However, it is a story wrought with challenges and heartache…

My father's death planted a seed of endless curiosity within me. At just five, I tried to model my mother's unbreakable spirit and found my own voice. I began helping her sell vegetables, sparking my entrepreneurial spirit and teaching me the true meaning of responsibility and service to others.

With just three years of formal education, my mother became a health worker, cloth designer, entrepreneur, midwife, and community leader known for her fearlessness and humanity. Her example inspired and instilled in me a deep commitment to serving others.

By age six, I campaigned for a space for children to play and learn in my mother's corner shop. This early passion for helping others set off a lifelong commitment to activism and deepened my appreciation for my mother's resolve.

Despite poverty, government oppression, societal expectations, and waves of natural disasters, my mother's steadfast belief in a person's innate abilities enabled me to persevere through unimaginable circumstances.

What happened to my family over the next several years reads like an epic drama, one in which the protagonist is constantly threatened, challenged, and persecuted. Yet, through it all, the protagonist tapped into an inner power that defied odds, transcended roadblocks, and ultimately led to a beautiful, fulfilling, abundant life.

IF YOU ARE KNOCKED DOWN SEVEN TIMES, GET UP EIGHT!

From an early age, I experienced the trauma of seeing our shantytowns repeatedly demolished by the government, forcing us to move multiple times, which fueled my resolve for justice.

By age eleven, driven by displacement, threats to my mother's shop—our livelihood—and instability in education, I joined year-long demonstrations against the oppressive government. Witnessing my mother rebuild our home, hearing stories of hardship, and absorbing our community's struggles inspired me to become a community activist. These experiences earned my community's trust to represent them in preserving our shantytown.

At thirteen years old, our country was devastated by historic floods, causing significant damage to essential resources like food, water, sanitation, and transportation, leading to another severe famine; shantytowns were particularly hard hit.

When the international community conducted airdrops, I found myself in a leadership position, coordinating with aid organizations to ensure the fair distribution of resources. This responsibility further solidified the community's trust in my ability to represent them in developing our shantytown.

These early experiences laid the foundation for my career advocating for human potential and empowering others to rebuild their lives. But not before I endured hardship, arrest, government abuse, and threats to my life. With resilience, no matter how many times we are knocked down, we keep standing.

RESILIENCE IN INJUSTICE

When I was eighteen, I was in a beauty salon when the police suddenly entered and arrested all the women present, accusing the salon of being illegally run. We were shoved into an open truck like cattle, and each time one of us asked why we had been arrested, we were met with beatings, insults, and threats. Silent tears streamed down our faces as we sat, each lost in our thoughts yet connected by a shared sense of confusion and injustice.

At that moment, my mother's image and her words lit up from the depths of my being.

"Be grateful we are still here; things can be demolished, but our essence, who we truly are, cannot be. Remember: who you truly are can't be destroyed."

My memory of her words gave me the strength to endure the arrest. No matter what happens to you or how much is taken from you, your soul cannot be demolished. Whether you're facing natural disasters, societal prejudice, or personal losses, your essence perseveres, and though you may feel shattered, it can never be destroyed.

This is the true power of resilience—it's not just about bouncing back but about the enduring strength of our deepest self.

In physical sciences, resilience means *"the power of returning to the original shape after compression."*

I believe resilience is the key to unlocking human potential. It is the pathway back to our identities. It is the seed of curiosity that empowers us to be hopeful and centered while seeking solutions.

And it is always a guiding light leading us home.

RESILIENCE ROOTED IN SELF-BELIEF

After I was released from jail, my mind replayed the events. A group of young women was arrested, dehumanized, detained, and fined simply for visiting a legitimate beauty salon. Worse, our families had to pay an amount they couldn't afford to secure our release from jail.

Although I didn't know what to do, the need to address these injustices became an ever-present drive, guiding my every thought and decision. Our shantytown was again facing the threat of forced eviction. Life was already a constant struggle. Our homes, built from whatever materials we could find, were vulnerable to rain, wind, heat, and natural disasters. I vividly remember nights when heavy floods turned our streets into rivers and our homes into soggy, leaking shelters.

As I replayed these harrowing events in my mind, I recalled a moment from my childhood when my mother stood up against armed government officers who tried to evict us. She faced them with unyielding strength and declared, "We have paid for this land multiple times, and we are not moving anymore." This memory ignited a deep fire within me.

I realized my determination and self-belief were rooted in these early lessons of resilience. My mother's actions taught me to honor our dignity, nurture our worth, and believe in our abilities. There will always be those who doubt you and circumstances that threaten to derail you. But if you're faithful to yourself and your abilities, you view those obstacles as minor setbacks. You see only possibilities and opportunities.

Nothing can interfere with a mission and vision fully fueled by your heart.

RESILIENCE ROOTED IN CORE VALUES

A couple of months after being released from jail, I ran into one of the hairdressers who was arrested with me. I asked how she and the others were doing. Her smile faded. "The beauty salon we worked at was shut down, leaving all of us jobless.

She shared that while she recently found work at a salon in another city, it required her to take four transportation connections. Plus, since buses didn't reach the shantytown, she had to walk long distances in the dark, which was extremely dangerous.

Her story haunted me. It reminded me of when I was six, trying to bring order to my life, watching children on the streets struggle to survive. I remembered how I created a safe corner at my mother's shop for us to play and learn. As these thoughts merged, a vision of creating a beauty salon flashed vividly before me. I envisioned a salon that would be more than just a place for beauty services; it would be a sanctuary to empower women to regain their dignity, support their families, and unlock their full potential. This vision became my driving force.

When I shared the idea with my mother, she said, "There is nothing you can't achieve. Learn the process and resolve to pay the price."

Your values aren't just a reflection of how you view right and wrong; they're a barometer that guides every decision you make. Defining your values nurtures resilience. These principles apply not only to individuals but also to businesses, organizations, communities, and nations. Values are your north star when life throws you off course and the roadmap that guides you to your true purpose. Sometimes, they require us to take a stand.

Little did I know that being arrested would lead to the creation of something that symbolized my journey—not only to foster inner strength but also to help others unlock their full potential. When you understand your values, they act as armor and oxygen, protecting you, guiding your authentic choices, and fostering the inner strength needed to unlock your true potential.

RESILIENCE ROOTED IN PERSEVERANCE

Throughout my life, I faced immense prejudice, including societal beliefs that people from my tribe were not meant for entrepreneurship, especially as a poor, young black woman. Reflecting on this, I realized why my mother was unwavering in her efforts to instill inner resilience in us. She knew that overcoming these barriers was essential for us to thrive.

To open a beauty salon, I needed a location with running water, electricity, and potential clients who could afford the services. This meant looking at properties in the city, where rent was exorbitant and required advance payment of up to a year.

After multiple rejections, I found a building owned by a church that was still under construction. My application was rejected numerous times because I couldn't afford to pay a year's rent in advance. Undeterred, I kept reapplying. I met with the board several times and, despite the rejections, persisted, working through various channels until I reached the bishop of the church.

After numerous attempts, he finally agreed to see me. I shared my vision and requested a recommendation letter from him to the board to allow me to pay the rent in installments. To show my commitment, I showed up at his office every morning on my way to work. My persistence paid off. Finally, he wrote a recommendation letter, and my application was approved.

When I shared the news with my mother, she was overjoyed and asked if the bishop mentioned anything about his past. I recalled that he had once been a teacher in a village. Her eyes lit up with recognition and she said, "I think I know him."

One day I encountered the bishop and described my mother. He remembered her and said, "Now I understand your courage and determination. She had the same qualities. I was saddened when she didn't return after the third-grade break because I knew she had a great future."

We cannot quit just because things get hard. Instead, we must remember why we started. As my mother said, it doesn't matter what other people think. What matters is what *you* see, what *you* believe, and what you are willing to strive for. Perseverance cultivates resilience. Resilience strengthens us, businesses, communities, and society to drive profound change.

RESILIENCE ROOTED IN DETERMINATION

My journey to secure a loan for the business began at a bank in the city, where I filled out extensive loan applications, which were quickly rejected. Undeterred, I approached multiple banks and was again turned down. Each rejection fueled my determination to persevere. One bank insisted I bring a guarantor, so my mother accompanied me.

We sat across from the banker, hopeful and eager, but he looked at us and said, "You're wasting your time, your mother's time, and other people's time." My mother smiled and said, "Son, you don't know who she truly is and what she's capable of. One day, I hope you hear about a young, black, skinny girl from a shantytown who owns a beauty salon. She will be the girl you said was wasting her time." On our way out, my mother turned to me and said, "This is how he sees you, but it is how you see yourself that matters.

It was clear that no bank would give me a loan, so a new idea flashed into my mind. I would help other customs clearance agents by typing and preparing their documents, which would provide a second stream of income I could use to fund the beauty salon. It worked!

This isn't just a story about securing a loan; it's about proving that with enough determination, belief, and action, one can overcome even the most entrenched prejudices. It's about relentlessly pursuing a vision that aligns with your mission. Each challenge I faced strengthened my inner resilience and deepened my commitment to finding solutions. Every "no" only fueled my determination and further nurtured my resilience.

GRAND OPENING DAY: NORA BEAUTY SALON

The day arrived for the grand opening of the salon. This was not just the launch of "Nora Beauty Salon," named after my youngest sister—it was a testament to our potential. The salon symbolized what could be achieved with resilience and determination.

Yet, this isn't the happy ending because success is not a linear journey. Less than two years after that grand opening, I received shocking news one night: the salon was on fire. The damage was severe, and my world collapsed.

My mother looked at me and said, "You're bigger than this fire, and you have the ability to rebuild it." During the rebuilding process, I focused on the vision that had inspired the salon in the first place: to empower women to regain their dignity, support their families, and uplift our community. Rebuilding was a powerful reminder that success is not a straight path but a series of challenges that test our resolve and commitment.

This chapter isn't just about the resilience needed to rebuild a business or home. It's about the resilience required to overcome any storm in life—whether it's health issues, relationship struggles, career setbacks, financial difficulties, or natural disasters. The fire that consumed our salon was both a literal and figurative trial by fire. It forced us to rebuild from the ashes, relying on inner strength, an unshakeable belief in my vision, and the unwavering support of my mother and community.

Today, I am an educator, activist, entrepreneur, personal transformation leader, coach, mentor, and speaker dedicated to empowering entrepreneurs and leaders to build lives of purpose, passion, and authenticity. I believe that resilience is the unbounded spirit within every individual that empowers us to unlock our full potential, live purposeful lives with dignity and grace, and contribute to the common good of society.

At the root of every success story stands resilience. Resilience can be tested but never broken. It can be threatened but never relinquished without our permission. With resilience, no matter what challenges life brings, or how daunting the path to success is, you will overcome and thrive with grace.

It is resilience that pieces together our broken parts, stands as a symbol of our spirit, and ultimately moves us forward again and again, pushing us closer to our destiny.

About Buthiana

Transformative Leader | Activist | Educator | Entrepreneur | Coach | Speaker

Buthiana's journey exemplified resilience from an early age, which took her from shantytowns to global leadership. After losing her father as a child and enduring harsh conditions, she discovered that inner strength is critical to overcoming obstacles and unlocking potential for success, inner peace, leadership, and more. Despite overwhelming hardship and oppression, she never lost hope, drawing strength from herself, her family, and her community.

At five Buthiana helped her mother sell vegetables to support their family, igniting an early entrepreneurial spirit. These formative experiences fueled her drive and enabled her to excel in the male-dominated customs clearance field as a teenager, inspiring many.

By age six Buthiana was advocating for children's needs in her community. These early initiatives helped facilitate international aid during crises as a teenager. Her leadership helped build her community and empowered over one thousand families. Her community activism and leadership led her to work with an NGO at age sixteen, providing personal development services. She quickly rose to lead one of the NGO's centers, empowering thousands of teachers, health workers, entrepreneurs, and community leaders.

In addition to her professional roles, Buthiana founded multiple businesses that inspired and empowered others. She also led a nonprofit focused on empowering communities. After a discriminatory law ended her customs clearance career, Buthiana launched a microfinance initiative that empowered hundreds of women.

Buthiana's initiatives foster growth across personal, professional, and communal domains, enabling individuals to thrive regardless of background. She passionately believes in the immense potential within everyone and in the power to unlock it.

Her achievements have earned her national and international recognition, including Toastmasters International's highest honor in leadership. She is also featured in the *Living Athena* book for exemplifying leadership. Buthiana believes true leadership is measured by the lives we touch and the change we inspire.

Living in the USA, Buthiana continues to inspire and empower individuals to rock their resilience for a purposeful, fulfilling life. Through coaching and speaking engagements, she helps people break free from limiting beliefs, fostering self-worth, inner peace, confidence, and self-motivation, regardless of background—all keys to transformation. Guided by her belief that resilience is the foundation of every success and leadership, Buthiana envisions a world where everyone is inspired to rock their resilience and transform their lives.

For coaching and speaking services, visit www.rockingyourresilience. com or email buthaina@rockingyourresilience.com. Follow on Facebook and Instagram: @rockingyourresilience.

CHAPTER 7

POWER HABITS!

How to Become the Best,
Healthiest Version of Yourself

By Robert Kelly, MD

My younger brother died from sudden arrhythmic death syndrome while I was in medical school. It was devastating for our family. He was a fit, active, healthy twenty-one-year-old.

After graduating from college and spending my early years working as a doctor in Ireland, I realized that I wanted to specialize in something acute with immediate life-saving results. Cardiology was the perfect match.

I also worked with defibrillator companies to raise awareness around sudden death, to teach resuscitation and bring defibrillators into sports clubs and the community. As years rolled on, I realized a desire to help as many adults as I could to prevent premature death, live longer, and enjoy happier, healthier lives. I chose people over thirty years of age who would be more exposed to chronic diseases, stroke, heart attacks and premature death.

One of the biggest lessons that I have learned throughout my twenty-year career journey is that our health is our most precious resource. Many people become ill if their body isn't healthy and yet, health and longevity do not begin in the body, but in the mind.

Don't believe me?

I hope you will.

Because the reality is almost one third of the people who read this book will die of heart disease or stroke. But you can tip the odds in your favor and add years to your life—if, that is, you heed the advice I'm about to share with you.

A Taste of My Own Medicine

I trained in cardiology in Ireland and the UK. My family and I then moved to North Carolina for five years, and I trained as an interventional cardiologist.

Upon returning to Ireland, I took up a job as a consultant cardiologist, and I helped manage acute heart attack patients at the local public hospital and built up my cardiology clinic at a private hospital.

This has been thoroughly enjoyable, very busy at times and hard work, but I have met incredible people, who let me into their lives, and I am so grateful to help so many to improve their health and stay well.

Listening to them remains my greatest source of learning. Their stories helped me to innovate and find new ways to improve their health, to understand their challenges and to explore what more I could do for them.

Many patients would struggle to lose weight, to find time for exercise, to sleep and to deal with stress. I discovered that there was never enough time in consultations to give them the information they needed and in truth giving them a booklet and encouraging them to change behaviors never made a huge difference. In fact, many patients returned with more problems than solutions at the follow up visits. What could I do?

An Unlikely Path Leads to Purpose

Between the 2009 recession in Ireland and the onset of the COVID pandemic in 2019, my practice experienced tremendous growth.

I had spent the recent years studying a more holistic approach to health, as I had noticed an alarming trend. Many patients were not heeding my advice and were coming back to me even bigger and less healthy. I realized that medicine and surgeries don't solve problems, *patients* do!

The reality is that if you are living a sedentary life filled with overwhelming stress, poor sleep, unhealthy diet, inactivity, smoking and drinking too much, then no pill or surgery can change that. We must make changes ourselves.

It was during those years that a colleague suggested I travel to a conference on lifestyle medicine. I hadn't heard of it, but I decided to go and was instantly hooked. Every factor of lifestyle medicine is backed by scientific evidence and closely related to cardiology. I knew it could help my patients, so I became the first accredited lifestyle medicine hospital consultant in Ireland.

My trainer at the gym suggested I investigate a Stanford professor named Dr. BJ Fogg. Dr. Fogg had created a method for behavior transformation called Tiny Habits. The idea is that small steps lead to big gains and that tiny habit changes are more sustainable and less intimidating than gigantic changes made all at once. I took his program and decided to incorporate the principles of it into my patients' treatment plans.

I was so passionate about the possibilities that lifestyle medicine held that I cofounded the Irish Society of Lifestyle Medicine with like-minded medical colleagues in Ireland.

In 2019 when COVID hit, there were so many people falling ill. It was a calamitous time. People were restricted from leaving their homes. Thousands were hospitalized and almost ten thousand people died. Worst of all many died alone in hospitals as family were unable to visit them. Everyone was struggling, and we all wanted to help each other cope and survive.

I was always interested in technology and digital health. COVID provided an opportunity to engage with people online. I decided to join the virtual bandwagon and set up my first webinar. So many people attended and shared their health struggles that I went on to develop a lifestyle program helping people to look after their own health and well-being, especially very busy homemakers and professionals (including healthcare workers).

I taught the pillars of lifestyle medicine and various techniques for manifestation and habit change, and it was a huge success.

I am deeply moved by the transformations that take place inside this program and the trust my patients place in me.

I have my first publication, *The Heart Book*, launching in September, and my hope is that it will help millions of people change their minds so they can change and lengthen their lives.

I hope you'll read it, but in the meantime here are some tips to get you started.

Change Happens First in the Mind

When I came back to Ireland in 2007, I weighed 210 pounds. I had worked long hours in North Carolina. I found that I skipped meals, and I snacked on ultra-processed food and coffee during the day when I could find free time. I wasn't getting much time either with my family and exercise was not high on my priority list.

One day a nutritionist approached me at work and asked if I'd be interested in joining forces. Together we would help people manage their weight. Not one to be a hypocrite, I finally got serious about my own body and our program helped me to release twenty pounds.

My energy skyrocketed, I felt amazing, my sleep quality improved, and I was much more productive during the day. I started golfing on weekends and spending more time with my family. Adopting just a few new habits of eating healthier and exercising had set off a ripple effect of positive change in my entire life!

What I know, however, is that none of those changes would have happened had I not first changed my mind. I had to change how I was thinking about my health journey. I had to stop seeing it as a negative and laborious sacrifice and start seeing it as a gift. I had to take responsibility and focus on my goal of making time for my self-care.

I had to begin to adopt the behavior of the person I wanted to be, a man who enjoyed a positive life and work blend, ate a healthy diet, took regular exercise, looked great, was close to his family, and made time to meet friends.

I found that when I began to leverage the power of visualization and engage my subconscious, it was easier to envision and embody the person I wanted to become.

Temptation and withdrawal were not a problem because the healthy version of me wasn't interested in toxic, high-fat food or doing work every day of the week.

I had a new identity that excited me. And I wasn't about to go backward!

How you think is directly proportional to what you ultimately do. Imagine the ideal version of yourself, and work to make the choices that the ideal version would make.

PAINT A PICTURE OF HEALTH

One of my favorite tools to teach my patients is to create a vision board.

It might sound out of the ordinary for a cardiologist to teach such a thing and at first, the concept was far outside my comfort zone.

Yet I came to discover that there is solid scientific evidence behind the use of vision boards as it involves several psychological and neurological concepts that influence focus and goal attainment.

When you create vivid mental images of your goals, it functions like the mental rehearsal techniques used by athletes to enhance performance. The brain often cannot distinguish between a real event and a vividly imagined one, which primes the brain to notice opportunities that can help achieve these goals. This priming effect is due to the brain's reticular activating system (RAS), which filters information and highlights what's important.

Furthermore, engaging with a vision board can reinforce neural pathways associated with the behaviors and actions needed to achieve goals, thanks to neuroplasticity, the brain's ability to reorganize itself by forming new neural connections.

To begin, choose images that represent an ideal version of your goals and visualize how you would feel if those goals came to fruition. Embody the identity of the person who would live the life represented on your vision board.

Just recently I called my vision board trainer in Canada to tell her I'd be participating in this book with Jack Canfield.

After congratulating me, she reminded me that this exact event was on a vision board I had shared with her four years earlier.

CREATE TINY HABITS

Creating tiny habits leverages the power of small, manageable actions to create lasting behavioral change. This method allows you to break big goals into small achievable steps so you change your daily routine without feeling overwhelmed.

Start by identifying a behavior you want to develop, and then shrink it down to its smallest possible version. For instance, if you want to establish a habit of daily exercise, begin with a single push-up or a short walk around the block. Next, anchor this tiny habit to an existing routine, such as doing a push-up right after brushing your teeth. Lastly, celebrate your success immediately so that the task is associated with a positive emotion.

I had one client who wanted to lose a significant amount of weight, but nothing seemed to work. The number she was trying to attain was intimidating and felt impossible. I encouraged her to let go of the number of pounds she wanted to lose and focus instead on eating two healthy meals a day.

It worked. Her focus shifted from this daunting number to something much more manageable, planning two healthy meals each day.

This is a method that can apply to absolutely anything. If the idea of writing a book overwhelms you, write one paragraph a day. If you are working to repair your marriage, say one kind thing a day.

The changes in habit are tiny, but the results are extraordinary.

Keep a record. Tracking your goals in writing is a highly effective strategy.

Writing things down transforms them from abstract ideas to concrete plans. Not only that, but science shows that writing engages parts of the brain that aid in memory retention and recall, which helps keep your goals at the forefront of your mind.

When a goal and the steps to achieving it are written, it serves as an accountability tool to which you can refer to and track your progress. It's a daily reminder of your objective when life gets busy or overwhelming.

One of my clients, an engineer, kept a detailed food diary to track his intake and used multiple journals, mind maps, and vision boards, one for each goal.

It worked. As of the time of this writing he has achieved most of his goals.

If there is something you want, write it down! If it's not in writing, it's not a goal; it's a wish.

LEVERAGE THE POWER OF A SUPPORT SYSTEM

Throughout my life, anytime I set a goal for myself, I found people to help me achieve it. Whether I attended a conference with like-minded colleagues or turned to my wife for accountability, I learned that success came faster and more easily when it was supported by and shared with people I trusted.

Support systems play a crucial role not just in goal achievement but also in health.

The correlation between social isolation and shorter lifespans is supported by extensive research in psychology, sociology, and medicine. Social isolation can lead to chronic stress, which triggers the body's fight-or-flight response.

This response when continually activated can cause long-term damage to your body.

People need people.

Cultivating meaningful relationships is perhaps one of the most important keys to living a longer, happier life.

The good news is that pets can deliver the same kind of health benefits. The key isn't who you're around, but rather what gifts they bring to your life. At the end of the day what's most important is that you find ways to infuse your life with more of these three things: companionship, accountability, and love.

NO ONE WOULD DO THE PUSH-UPS FOR ME

I live a very busy life just like millions of people all over the world. I have learned to better manage my time so that I prioritise my self-care and then work.

I have found a balance and created a successful and meaningful life. I am prioritizing myself, playing golf (and winning!), and spending quality time with family and friends. I am happier than ever. But no one handed it to me. I realized very early on in my health and life journey that no one would do the work for me. I had to want it badly enough to make changes and step into a new authentic version of myself that felt strong, healthy and unstoppable.

Along the way I have treated thousands of patients whom I am so grateful to for sharing their stories of success. I like to give people hope, no matter what their diagnosis is. Heart disease is preventable, treatable and in some cases reversible. I empower patients to achieve this. I want patients to be and stay well, and to live long, enjoyable lives free of significant disease.

I still slip up. I might be a doctor, but I'm also a human! The key is to forgive yourself for the slipup and immediately recommit to the healthy lifestyle you've chosen.

Believe in yourself.

No matter where you are right now, or how much you weigh, or what the medical chart says, there is always hope.

As you're reading this, you have within you a powerful seed of potential.

Let it grow. For as you water it with intention, action, and perseverance, you will find that the small seed grows into a completely transformed mind, a healthy body, and a happy, fulfilling life!

About Robert

Robert Kelly, MD, is an internationally acclaimed Intervention Cardiologist and Lifestyle Medicine Physician who has combined these areas to deliver a holistic approach to heart health.

He is an engaging, motivating and entertaining public speaker and has given talks and training to patients, professionals, corporates, colleagues, students and parents all over the world. He has a passion for preventing heart attacks and strokes by helping people to make lasting lifestyle changes. His approach is based on coaching small steps for sustained behavior change.

He is an Associate Professor of Clinical Medicine at UCD, a senior lecturer in Lifestyle Medicine at RCSI. He is a cofounder of the Irish Society of Lifestyle Medicine and a board member of The European Society of Lifestyle Medicine. He is a fellow of faculty of sport and exercise medicine, American College of Cardiology, Royal College of Physicians in Ireland, European Society of Cardiology. He trained in cardiology at the University of North Carolina, USA.

Robert runs Cardiology & Lifestyle Medicine clinics at Beacon Hospital, Dublin, Ireland.

He has an MBA from Henley Business School, UK. He is a Certified Tiny Habits coach, a behavior designer, and a Jack Canfield Success Principles coach.

His health programs have helped hundreds of patients release weight, improve exercise, lower stress, sleep better, stop smoking and find more energy and vitality to enjoy life. These behaviors are known to prevent, treat and potentially reverse heart disease. Several patients have been able to reduce their heart medications as well. Professional clients have reported greater job satisfaction, better job engagement and performance after doing the programs.

Robert has appeared on TV and radio and in national and international media, discussing heart health, lifestyle, mindset, habits, and health behavior change.

He is the author of a forthcoming book, *The Heart Book*, and was a TEDx speaker in October 2024.

Robert lives in Dublin, Ireland. He enjoys family time with his wife,

Lorna; three children; and dog, Holly, as well as playing golf and padel tennis, walking, traveling, and socializing with friends.

Connect with Robert:

www.linkedin.com/in/drrobertkelly
www.instagram.com/drrobertkelly
www.facebook.com/drrobertkelly
www.tiktok.com/@dr.robert.kelly
www.drrobertkelly.ie
www.beaconhospital.ie

CHAPTER 8

THE ART OF REINVENTION

Cultivating Habits of High Achievers

By Annette Dowdle

The news reports were grim, but none of us could have imagined that it would be one of the most devastating events in our history.

I lived in the New Orleans metro area with my husband, our twin one-year-olds, and a six-year-old, and one thing was clear: Hurricane Katrina was coming our way. When the order to evacuate came, we headed to Dallas to stay in a hotel, believing we'd be back in a few days. But as Katrina ravaged our city, the grim reality set in. We were not going home anytime soon. So we headed to Alabama, where my husband and I grew up, to be with family.

We had brought our babysitter and her two kids with us and were all crammed together in my mother's small house. Still, we were better off than most families, whose lives were reduced to just a few belongings as they were ushered into an arena with thousands of others, a situation that brought out both the best and worst of humanity. We watched the news in horror, our adopted city submerged under water and people clinging to rooftops awaiting rescue. There was no water and no electricity, and the haunting sight of bodies being carried away by the currents was something out of a nightmare. We had no idea if our home was still standing, and it was clear that the road to restoration would be long and uncertain.

When we returned home three weeks later, it looked like a third-world country. No electricity, no 911 services, no water. We did the best we could to keep things normal for the kids, but deep down I knew that life could not go back to business as usual.

LIFE INTERRUPTED

I've always been a hard worker. I was a good student and right after college secured a great job with a national insurance company. Eventually, my husband and I decided to move to Louisiana. It was a great time for me, as I continued to have success in my career and gave birth to my three children. But Katrina drew a clear line in the sand. Life and industry were completely interrupted. I had no idea if I would still have a job. I watched some of my friends navigate devastating losses of property and it hit me that life was indeed short and totally unpredictable.

I had to ask myself, was I living it the way I wanted to?

Sure, I had a job and a family, and was grateful for that, but like a lot of people, I was in default mode. My calendar was packed, my routine was set, and I didn't stop to think too much about whether I was living a life on purpose or on autopilot.

I decided to take an inventory of my life and what I found was that it felt small. Often when we have enough food and healthy kids, we trick ourselves into thinking we should be satisfied. We should be *grateful*, but we don't have to become complacent. I wanted a bigger life. I wanted a house on the golf course and another at the beach. I dove deep into personal development work, studying the work of the world's most prolific coaches and the habits of the world's most notable millionaires. I adopted their routine and before long, I had my two houses, the car I wanted, and had accomplished several of my biggest goals.

That's the thing about life, though—it changes on a dime.

2021 marked one of the worst years of my life.

My husband and I had both traveled throughout our entire marriage, but when COVID hit, we were stuck at home with one another and realized that we'd grown apart. I tried to make it work, but after a year of walking on eggshells and zero growth, it was time to walk away. Shortly after the divorce, my mother fell, hit her head and died suddenly. My sister was diagnosed with liver and lung cancer and my father had to be placed in assisted living and eventually died.

All of this in just one year.

I fell into a very dark place. For so long I had carried the flag of resilience, convincing myself that I could handle anything, but 2021 knocked the wind out of me. Then Christmas came. I was sitting alone during the holidays missing my parents. The kids were at my husband's girlfriend's house and the silence was deafening. I was overcome with emotion and realized I was at a crossroads. I could wallow in these losses, or I could return to the habits that helped me piece my life back together after Katrina. That's exactly what I did.

Today, I am once again living a life of abundance. I love my career as an insurance producer with a phenomenal company. I host a podcast on leadership called "Elevate" and have participated in multiple leadership programs and boards. I've had the chance to work with Jack Canfield and am now writing a book on leadership/culture based on my real-life career experiences with clients.

Returning to the habits of millionaires had now twice pulled me out of darkness. These simple habits, written about for ages, were in fact the key to rebuilding my life.

You probably already know what these habits of success and manifestation are. You can maybe even recite them. And that's precisely why you may be ignoring them altogether.

THE GAP BETWEEN KNOWING AND DOING

If you've ever read books such as *The 7 Habits of Highly Successful People* or *The Millionaire Morning*, what you'll notice is that none of the wisdom offered is rocket science. It's also not all that unique. Yet human behavior is predictable at this point.

Studies show that people need to hear things at least seven

times before they sink in. Yet there's a risk in that, as the more we see something, the less likely we are to pay attention to it. Think of how often you drive the same route and are so accustomed to how things look that you don't even notice that a store has changed hands. Or you scroll through social media and are bombarded with so many ads that your eyes grow blind to them.

The same is true for the barrage of personal development advice out there that all teach some version of the same principles. They all impart the same general conventional wisdom, and they do it because we need them to! We need things to be constantly reinforced so that when the time is right, we will move from ignoring the lessons, to reading them, to actually living them.

Conventional wisdom becomes conventional through precedent, meaning that enough people have tried something and experienced the same result, that we can draw a universal conclusion. Most of the world's millionaires have adopted certain practices and they credit these practices with helping them reach new heights of success. It has worked often enough that we now have lists of things to do if we want to emulate their success.

You don't need to spend money on these things or be born into them. You simply need to go beyond skimming the list and absorbing it, applying it and making it a way of life.

For me, these practices helped me manifest everything I want in life.

So now I challenge *you*. Read these habits. Practice them for just six weeks, and watch what happens next.

TREAT YOUR BODY KINDLY

It should be common sense, right? Yet most people don't do it. Exercise and eating healthy are habits of millionaires because the most successful people understand the impact these practices have on their productivity, mental clarity, and longevity.

Maintaining a healthy body enhances energy levels, reduces stress, and improves focus, enabling them to perform at their best.

Also, these habits cultivate discipline and commitment, qualities essential for achieving and sustaining success. By prioritizing their health, millionaires invest in their most valuable asset: *themselves.*

Exercising and eating right are not just a smart idea; they are an act of self-love.

Practice Gratitude

You've heard this one before and maybe even railed against it when life got tough, and the list of things to be thankful for felt painfully short. But research in positive psychology shows that practicing gratitude dramatically increases your energy, your mental health and your motivation for tackling what life throws at you.

Gratitude shifts the focus from what's lacking to what's present, and if you understand the law of attraction, you know how important that is. For me, 2021 seemed to send more to grieve than to be thankful for, but as I made the commitment to healing, I knew I had to find something to be grateful for. I gave thanks for my children, my own healthy body, the roof over my head and every bite of food or ray of sunshine. You can always find something to appreciate and the more you pour your energy into appreciating life's blessings, the more blessings life sends your way.

Set Inspiring Goals

One of my favorite books is *The Compound Effect* by Darren Hardy. In it he writes, "Forget about willpower. It's time for whypower. Your choices are only meaningful when you connect them to your desires and dreams." Darren teaches that you make your choices and then your choices make *you.*

Life is fueled by our dreams and desires. Our days are made up of the steps we take to move towards those dreams. That's why one of the most common pieces of advice for treating depression is to have a goal. Goals give us purpose and the steps to achieving our goals give us structure. Millionaires not only have goals, but they also have an unwavering belief in their own ability to turn a goal into a reality and one of the methods they use to cultivate that belief is visualization.

Years ago I decided to run a marathon. I was not a runner but wanted to challenge myself. I visualized every mile on the marathon route. I was super specific in my visualization, picturing what the clock would show as my time and where each water station would be. In my mind, I watched myself crossing the finish line. It worked so well that I brought the practice of visualization into my professional life, and doing so has helped me increase my income exponentially.

Think about it. Every single invention started as an idea. Someone had a goal, pictured the invention complete in their mind, mapped out steps to make it happen and imagined what the successful completion would feel like. The phone you're holding, the chair you're sitting on, the light above your head were all the result of goals, visualizations and of course, *action!*

FIND YOUR MASTERMIND

They say you're the average of the five people you hang out with the most.

They also say that if you're the smartest person in the room, you're in the wrong room. None of us knows exactly who "they" are, but I think we can agree that if there are thousands of quotes around the importance of who you surround yourself with, it's true!

I've learned to be very intentional about who I spend time with and have had to cut people out of my life whose influence held me back. It isn't easy, but when you consider that everyone around you is leaking energy, and that the leaked energy will inevitably spill onto you, you'll want to make sure what lands on you isn't toxic! One of the best ways to make sure the energy around you is clean and beneficial is to curate your own mastermind.

Most millionaires have a mastermind because it provides a

powerful support network of like-minded individuals who offer diverse perspectives and constructive feedback. Your mastermind doesn't have to be a group of the world's brilliant minds. Having even one person to brainstorm with is a powerful catalyst for growth.

I have an accountability partner, and we speak every week, no matter how busy we both are. We share our goals and hold each other's feet to the fire when packed calendars threaten to pull us off track.

My accountability partner and I met through a mastermind group that our company encouraged us to form back in July 2019. This group walked with me on my journey through the darkness and back to the light of today. I feel blessed that we connected at just the right time and endured challenges together as the world navigated COVID.

Find your tribe, even if your tribe is one person you text once a week for a combination of love, support and a kick in the butt! There's power in collective wisdom. And of course, as "they" say, two heads are better than one.

Take Regular Inventory

One of the first books I ever read on success and personal development is *The Power of Positive Thinking*. For a long time I would hop on and off the train, thinking positively when life was going well and abandoning that ship when it wasn't.

Eventually I got it. The key to healing, success and manifesting everything I wanted in life depended on thinking positively even during the darkest times. It's a muscle you must develop, but once you do, you'll find that you're able to dramatically shorten the time lapse between light and dark, between happy and sad, between pain and healing, and between failure and success.

There's another habit that the most successful millionaires in the world share that I haven't covered yet, but it is arguably the most important. They are deeply in touch with a higher power. It might be God, or the universe, or some energetic frequency that cannot be seen but is undoubtedly working behind the scenes to align us to our destinies.

The most successful people hold a connection to a higher power because it is invincible. The economy can collapse, inflation can rise, natural disasters can hit, but the one thing that can never be destroyed is our inner world—that connection to something bigger, that seed of hope that shows up in the darkest times, that tiny voice inside that urges us to keep going even in the face of tremendous loss.

If you have that source of power within you, you have everything you need to succeed. And if life's ups and downs bury your faith for a while, turn to the habits of the world's most successful people. They know a thing or two. Treat your body well, set goals that light you up, give thanks for what you already have, find your tribe, and when life goes south, remember this: We don't succeed by never failing but by rising each time we fall, committing to powerful habits, and investing in the one thing that will always have the highest return—*ourselves.*

About Annette

Annette Dowdle has dedicated over twenty-five years to excelling in business development, leadership, and sales. Throughout her career she has collaborated with hundreds of entrepreneurs and professionals nationwide, focusing on optimizing business performance and innovative cost containment strategies while building a better culture.

Annette holds the position of senior vice president at HUB International, where she works with a highly talented and skilled team responsible for managing all aspects of employee benefits programs. Her leadership is instrumental in developing cost-containment strategies and enhancing benefits to better meet the needs of their employees. Driven by a commitment to finding a better way, Annette's strategies are both innovative and impactful.

As the host of the recently launched podcast *Elevate with Annette*, she engages with business owners and entrepreneurs to explore leadership and work-life balance, offering valuable insights and strategies to enhance professional growth. Annette is also preparing to release her new book, *The Power of a Healthy Culture*, which promises to influence her field.

Annette also enjoys an active lifestyle traveling, skiing, hiking, paddle-boarding, attending morning yoga sessions, and going out on the water with family and friends.

Connect with Annette Dowdle on social media to stay updated on her work. Follow her podcast @elevatewithannettedowdle, subscribe to her YouTube channel, find her on Instagram @annette.dowdle, and connect with her on LinkedIn.

Email annette.dowdle@hubinternational.com for more information.

CHAPTER 9

HINDSIGHT

From Reflection to Transformation

By Earl Waud

The smell of antiseptic hangs in the air as the doctors wheel me to the surgery room. The steady beeping of the heart monitor mimics the ticking of the clock, counting down the seconds as the anesthesia kicks in.

I feel calm, as it's routine shoulder surgery, and I'm further reassured by the kind and confident eyes peeking out above the masked faces of the doctors standing over me.

I feel my eyelids grow heavy and my vision begin to blur as the world around me becomes distant and muffled.

As consciousness slips away, the harsh lights of the hospital room give way to an entirely different scene. A beautiful building materializes and on the door is a sign that reads "The Bureau of Hindsight." I open the door, and I'm greeted by a friendly receptionist, who already knows my name and why I've come. Over the next few hours I meet three people who introduce me to hindsight stones, seven stones that transport me back through my life's memories, offering the opportunity to relive precious moments and learn new lessons.

It's a beautiful experience, and as I feel myself begin to wake up, the three mentors deliver one last directive: Write a book; share this experience; help people change their lives.

I had never thought of writing a personal-development book. I'd written three technical books at that point, with no plans to expand my writing horizons. Yet as I began to wake from the surgery, I felt an urgent need to remember everything I had seen in my dream.

I went home and immediately set about writing what would become a highly acclaimed book called *Hindsight: The 7 Keys to Living Your Best Life.*

Since then I've written more books, become a speaker and a dedicated mentor, and devoted my life to my passion for understanding and championing human potential. Some of my clients and colleagues refer to me as The Hindsight Mentor.

You see, what I've realized is that my subconscious visit to the Bureau of Hindsight was not just a dream and it isn't just a story. It is a powerful tool for leveraging the transformational wisdom that all our life circumstances have to offer. Have you ever found yourself wishing you could go back in time and relive your most compelling moments? Or perhaps wishing for a chance to respond differently to a current situation? You can! And in that hindsight journey, you can reframe those moments, learn from them and use the new information to help you reframe your perspective, choose differently going forward and ultimately, uncover the secrets to your own potential.

The Bureau of Hindsight might also be called the School of Continuous Learning because that's what it offers—an ongoing course in self-discovery that reveals to you why you do what you do, how you make decisions and ultimately, what drives you to love, heal and succeed.

There are multiple levels of learning and each of them gifts us with insights we can use to fashion our most fulfilling lives. But it requires our willingness to pay attention to both our brains and our minds.

Many people think of the brain and the mind as one entity, but they are separate.

The brain is the physical organ responsible for regulating bodily processes and processing information. In contrast, the mind is abstract, and encompasses thoughts, emotions, consciousness, and desires. When you treat both your mind and your brain as partners in potential, the possibilities for joy and success are endless. And you do that by learning.

The most successful people understand that continuously learning is vital to a well-rounded and fulfilling experience of life. And the best part? There's no barrier to entry.

Anyone can embark on this journey at any time. And you don't even have to have shoulder surgery to do it!

What We Can Learn from Toddlers

Have you ever spent a day with a toddler? If so, you've witnessed their endless curiosity, and maybe been at the receiving end of a barrage of questions.

Toddlers love to ask, "Why?"

They want to know more.

They love to touch things they shouldn't.

Their eyes widen at every new experience and their spirits eagerly embrace every new adventure, whether it's as big as Disney World or as small as touching a snail for the first time.

We can learn a lot from their bottomless thirst for knowledge and their perseverance. The block tower tumbles, they rebuild it again and again until they find a solution.

Very often when someone is sharing a challenge they're having, I notice they're operating from a fixed mindset. They have a fixed perspective on what the problem is and why it happened, and they've convinced themselves that there's no solution. Essentially, they've blocked their brain from forming new possibilities.

Imagine if instead, every time you bumped into a challenge you treated it with great curiosity, like a mystery needing to be solved, rather than a cosmic punishment sent to sabotage you! Imagine if every day, you saw each moment and each conversation as an opportunity to learn something about yourself.

Learning is quite simply defined as the acquisition of knowledge. And of course, knowledge is power.

So, how powerful would you like to become?

Learn Your Way to Abundance

There are two levels of continuous learning I'd like to cover in this chapter. The first is practical.

Practical learning is the acquisition of skills and information. As toddlers, the entire world is an education, but over the years our definition of "learning" is diluted down to what happens between the walls of a school. Sadly, for most people learning stops when they graduate high school or college.

In fact, studies show that 33 percent of people never read a book again after high school!

Now that's not to say that books are the only way to learn, but it makes me wonder how many people lose a little passion for learning with each passing year of their life.

I've always been a student of personal development. I was intrigued by the concepts taught in books such as *Think and Grow Rich*, *The Magic of Thinking Big*, and *Awaken the Giant Within*. A few years ago someone posted a single ticket on eBay to a live Tony Robbins event in London. I snatched it up! I was blown away. So much so that after that, I purchased full price tickets for my entire family to attend his next U.S. event. The mindset lessons I learned there have helped shape my career, strengthen my relationships and help me effectively lead teams and coach clients.

What I know for sure is you can learn more to earn more.

The more you know, the more opportunities become available to you. I'm a big believer in being a lifelong student. I was working in network security when the pandemic hit. The company I was working with laid off more than seven hundred people, and I was one of them. Millions of people lost their jobs that year, which meant millions of people were all in the job market vying for the same positions!

I had a new job in less than two months, and I attribute that to my willingness to always be learning. I had studied current and relevant trends, and that knowledge helped me navigate the interview process with confidence.

Knowledge becomes a tool in your toolbox that is always readily available to you. The interview process would have been intimidating if I didn't have that technical knowledge in my pocket.

Whether you're educating yourself on your industry or reading up on current events, practical learning saves you from awkward silences, positions you as an authority and instills in you the confidence to speak, lead and take your place in whatever rooms you want to be in.

Not only that, but knowledge is a lifeline in social settings, high stakes meetings and even dangerous situations.

Spend ten minutes on Google, and you'll find hundreds of stories of people who survived life-threatening situations because they remembered something they read or saw on television.

So, you see? Learning doesn't just help you win at *Jeopardy*. It can land you jobs, make you the most interesting person in the room, and even save your life.

And that's just the basic level of learning. That's just the field of intellect.

What lies *beyond* the edges of intellectual knowledge is a deep and powerful invitation to know oneself.

UNWRAP THE GIFT

When I was writing the book *Hindsight*, it was meant to be a gift to others, but I quickly realized that it was an opportunity for me to more deeply understand myself.

It was a chance to relive pivotal moments in my life and reflect on where they led, what I learned and how the outcomes shaped me into who I am today.

I'm sure if you took a few minutes to think about the most important moments of your life, you might be taken for quite a ride! For most of us, what stands out as important coincides with what was life changing.

You may think of moments of joy like the birth of your children and moments of fear and uncertainty, like life-threatening situations or a painful divorce. Whether the moments that come to mind are happy or sad, they hold a lesson. If, that is, you have the courage to go on that journey and "meet" the moment again.

When the plot for *Hindsight* materialized, I revisited the birth of my daughter. It was one of the most joyous moments of my life, but I realized in *hindsight* that the overwhelming feeling of that moment was *gratitude*.

That taught me that gratitude is a gateway to joy. Now, when I need a joy infusion, I know to look for things I feel grateful for. That's just one example of how we can learn through hindsight.

Or how about this one? How many times have you looked back on a situation that went south and said to yourself, "I *knew* that was going to happen. I had a bad feeling, and I knew it was going to be a disaster!"

Hopefully reliving that moment in which you ignored your intuition is a lesson. Now you know what your intuition feels like, how it speaks, the physical sensations it comes with and you're less likely to ignore it again.

Everything that happens, happens *for* us.

It's a lesson, a warning, or a clue that acts like a breadcrumb leading us to a deeper understanding of our own hearts and minds.

Every day we have a choice—let each moment pass, or let each moment teach. Let each moment fade into oblivion, or let it gift us with another layer of wisdom, love, and armor against life's challenges.

The moment is always giving. You need only open your arms and your mind and take what it offers.

BORROW A BELIEF

As the desire to shift from my technical job to coaching and speaking grew, so did my hesitation.

I'd written multiple technical books and delivered talks about technical things, so I was already an experienced speaker. However, moving into the personal development realm felt like a steep and giant leap!

I attended a live training with Jack Canfield and his CEO Patty Aubery. During that training, each of us participating had to get up on stage and deliver a talk. Jack and Patty noticed my trepidation and poured words of encouragement into me. After my talk, Jack said that what I did was pretty much a master class in how to do a presentation. I was floored! I was hoping for great feedback, but deep down I hadn't expected it. The amount of belief that Jack poured into me flipped a switch.

I had started out needing to borrow *his* belief in me when I didn't yet have enough belief in myself.

Not long after that, my daughter drew me a picture. It was a butterfly and on it she wrote, "You can borrow my belief in you until you find your own."

I went on to write a second book called *Borrowed Belief.*

When you have a desire, a challenge or some other important task in your life and you don't believe you can achieve it, look outside of yourself. Speaking to a mentor or even reading a book about someone who has overcome an extraordinary feat can cause a kind of osmosis. Soon, their strength, their confidence and their conviction become your own.

Borrow a belief, store it in your heart, and keep borrowing until you're so full of belief in yourself, that nothing can stop you from achieving your dreams.

The DNA of Greatness

I've always been fascinated by my teachers' teachers. Imagine an entire lineage of greatness and wisdom passed down and built upon for hundreds of years. I've studied the lineage that connects some of the greatest minds in the world such as Jim Rohn, Jack Canfield, Bob Proctor, and Earl Nightingale.

Each mentor in this line is like a key that unlocks another door, leading you further into a labyrinth of wisdom

But sometimes your greatest mentor is yourself.

You aren't even close to reaching the peak of your knowledge and potential. Not because it's an unreachable summit, but because as soon as you reach the top of one mountain, I hope you'll find higher ones to climb. When you commit to continuous learning as a way of life, you get to wake up every day knowing that when you close your eyes at night, you'll be an even better version of yourself than you were the day before.

John Adams said, "There are two educations. One should teach us how to make a living, and the other, how to live."

That's why I commit to fueling both my brain and my mind. For me, gratitude has always been my strongest foundation. What I've found is that in life's valleys, when everything feels hard and gratitude is tough to come by, learning is a life raft. When solutions elude me, I know I can drink in the wisdom of a book. I can borrow belief from a friend. I can seek out a mentor and let their strength and experience spill over onto me.

And then a funny thing happens. I become the holder of wisdom for someone else. I become a thread in the lineage and a branch in the tree of knowledge.

Today, I lend my belief to you. Go ahead and borrow it for as long as you need to. Take a trip to the Bureau of Hindsight. Revisit your life's most powerful moments. The lessons you can learn from more deeply knowing yourself are like souvenirs you can keep forever.

Except unlike a seashell or postcard that simply remind you of a trip already taken, life's wisdom prepares and empowers you for the wild adventures and great successes yet to come!

About Earl

Earl Waud, celebrated as the ultimate Master of Change, is a driving force in personal development and transformation. His life is a testament to resilience, creativity, and unwavering commitment to excellence and continuous self-improvement.

Earl's mission of helping others achieve their full potential shines through his books, coaching, and mastermind programs. He specializes in reigniting the passion of individuals who have set their goals aside, people who are behind on their dreams, providing clarity and guidance to help them achieve their aspirations, increase their earnings, and love their life again.

Earl drives change for himself and the world. He holds two patents for groundbreaking inventions that revolutionized the software industry. As an author, Earl has written numerous books on life-changing topics, including several under the pen name Robert Anson, such as:

- *Purely Delicious*, an acclaimed gluten-free/dairy-free cookbook
- *Paws and Effect*, a comprehensive guide for dog parents
- *Healthy Aging*, insights for improving health and well-being in later years
- *Fibromyalgia and You*, helping those with this debilitating illness live their best life

Earl helped his daughter Madison become a published author with her heartwarming children's book, *Noah's Walk*, and now assists others in writing and publishing their books to share their stories and change the world.

His personal-development books, *Hindsight* and *Borrowed Belief*, have inspired countless readers to implement significant positive life changes. Earl is passionately working on his most important project yet, *Hindsight for Teens*, aimed at reducing teen suicide.

A lifelong learner, Earl continues to study with expert mentors to elevate his expertise. Recently, he unlocked his creative side, producing more than twenty stunning landscape oil paintings. His dedication to self-improvement extends to athletics, completing eight in-person marathons.

Continually pushing his limits, Earl has also finished multiday virtual distance events, covering more than 760 miles.

Earl resides in Texas with his wife, Patti, to whom he has been married for thirty-three years. Together they have raised three daughters, embodying the values of love, commitment, and perseverance. Additionally, Earl and Patti are devoted dog parents to three furry family members.

Earl Waud is committed to empowering individuals to achieve their dreams and lead fulfilling lives. His inspiring journey, coupled with his expertise and genuine desire to help others, makes him uniquely qualified to help people make the positive changes they desire.

Do you want help to live your best life? Contact Earl at www. TheHindsightMentor.com.

CHAPTER 10

BREAKING FREE

Transforming Pain into Power!

By Helene Kelly

"You will know that it's time to take your power back when there is no other viable choice."
—Brianna Wiest, When You're Ready,
This Is How You Heal

'm three years old and very proud of the little white sailor dress I'm wearing. My mother just bought it for me, and it's the perfect dress for a trip to the park with my uncle.

We found a sunny spot, totally secluded and surrounded by the tallest evergreen trees I'd ever seen. I'm lying on the soft grass, looking up at the blue sky, when suddenly my uncle is standing over me.

I'm confused because he's blocking the sun, but then he tells me what we're going to do next.

"Spread your legs."

I shot up from the bed, reeling from what I thought was a horrific nightmare but would soon discover it was something much worse.

It was a memory.

I was thirty-six years old when the memory of that trauma resurfaced. Until then I'd lived what felt like an average successful life.

I did well in school and attended Emerson college, graduating magna cum laude. I went on to work in PR and ad agencies and built a successful career. I had three luxury cars and an expensive home on three acres within a short walk to a private beach.

I took the leap and with just $5,000 left in my savings account, launched my own agency. That was almost thirty years ago, and it's still going strong. On paper life was great. I wasn't yet aware of what lurked under the surface.

My (first) husband and I began to have marital issues. I'd grown up believing in "till death do us part" and was willing to try anything to save our marriage.

It was during this time that I started to drink wine. A lot. At first, I drank after work, then *during* work lunches. Finally, I came to depend on wine as a coping mechanism.

Even our most buried pain eventually claws its way to the surface. Soon I was drinking so much I thought it might kill me.

I joined a twelve-step program and got sober, and since my husband refused to go to marriage counseling, I decided to go myself—to avoid a divorce. During one appointment the therapist asked me questions about myself. I told her about my life and went home to lay down. It was then that the vision of my uncle standing over me came rushing back to my memory.

I was obviously troubled by what I still thought might be a random, intrusive thought, so I called her and left a message.

During my next therapy appointment she played the message I'd left. Through the machine I heard my words but in a child's voice. It was deeply disturbing to hear myself describing the memory in a little girl's voice. She assured me this can happen as part of a dissociative response; that trauma victims can revert to a younger state of mind when expressing suppressed feelings.

It was the start of a decade of therapy and memory retrieval sessions that unveiled years of abuse by my uncle. My marriage didn't survive.

There were days I didn't think I could go on. There were days I wanted to skip therapy.

But the floodgates had been opened wide, and one thing was clear: The only way out was *through*.

TURNING RAGE INTO STRENGTH

I'd be lying if I said I was eager to tell my story.

I'm a successful business owner, but I'm also human. Of course, I wondered if people would view me differently.

But then it occurred to me…I hope they do. I hope their picture of me broadens from highly successful strategist to brave, unconquerable badass!

You see, what I know now is that trauma, while life altering, does not have to be a life sentence.

One in four women have been sexually assaulted. If you're at dinner with four friends, one of you has probably been a victim.

But most people suffer with that secret alone for a lifetime. We keep it suppressed because the pain of facing it is too great. We hide it because the perpetrators are still alive. We hide it because we don't want to be pitied or viewed as a freak.

I don't judge anyone else's journey. We all have our own timelines and our own catalysts for healing. But for me?

I was done keeping this secret.

The shame isn't mine, it's his.

What *is* mine, is the story of resilience, healing and success.

If you've ever experienced the shocking volt of pain and if you've been carrying it with you for far too long, I hope you read this story and realize that you can go on to live a healthy, happy life not in spite of your experiences but *because* of them.

It's those of us who have walked through the fire who come out the other side with superhuman empathy and a fierce determination to fight for what's right.

Years ago when I was working in the male-dominated world of PR and advertising, I hadn't yet opened Pandora's box of memories and yet, inside me was a primal instinct that would not allow my boundaries to be trespassed.

If a man disrespected me, an indescribable rage would bubble up. It was an overreaction for sure, but an understandable one, and once I learned to transform that rage into strength, I was unstoppable.

In one of the agencies I worked for, one of my male coworkers repeatedly undermined me. When I finally had enough and spoke up to him, he leaned into me, within inches of my face, and whispered something despicable and threatening.

I was silent, but knew it was time for me to stand up for myself, even if it meant losing my job. At that moment, I knew I was no longer a victim; I was the victor.

I marched right to the president's office and demanded action. Their response was to sweep it under the rug, so I called the Department of Labor and filed a formal complaint.

Rage left to fester can cause disease, but rage transformed becomes *strength*.

When you learn to channel intense emotions into constructive actions not only do you release the negativity from your own body and mind, but you become a catalyst for change.

Making the decision to stand as a symbol of survival is a powerful form of healing. It helps you recover your worth, your backbone, your voice and your very soul.

True transformation begins when your heart finally recognizes that what it's desperately seeking isn't vindication but healing and self-love. When you believe you're worth it, you'll fight for yourself.

TRANSFORMING A PAINFUL MEMORY INTO A SUCCESSFUL, HAPPY LIFE

The trauma I experienced as a child was horrifying, but I don't believe in degrees of trauma. Pain is pain. Yours may have been in the form of an ugly divorce, the loss of a friendship or the death of a loved one.

The definition of the word "trauma" in the dictionary is "a deeply distressing experience and the emotional shock that follows."

Any experience that shakes you to your core is traumatic, but the good news is that it is emotionally based, and emotions can be managed.

Today, I run a very successful marketing communications agency and serve multi-million-dollar clients. I also mentor women who have survived trauma and help them rebuild their lives.

If healing is your goal, here's a proven framework:

1. Work toward wholeness.

Most of the time when our lives have been ravaged by a traumatic experience, we save ourselves from the pain by pushing it down, and then layering numbing mechanisms on top of it. For me, wholeness could only be found by ridding myself of every mood-altering substance that was preventing me from knowing my true self; a divine creation.

Some people turn to food, shopping, gambling, sex, drugs or other numbing activities to escape the pain.

I remember thinking if I could just cut out the trauma with a surgical knife, I'd be normal again.

What I know now is that normal is subjective. There's no such thing. And while the memory may never go away, the impact it had on my life could.

It's not easy. When you commit to giving up your coping mechanisms, you will be forced to truly *feel*. It's brutal. The first things you'll feel are rage and shame and hurt. But here's the thing: Eventually you'll also feel love and joy and gratitude. When you stop burying what must be processed, you'll realize that the wall you built may have kept the pain out, but it kept out all the good stuff too.

And it's time to let in the light that has always been there for you.

2. Find replacements.

When I first made the decision to give up the things I was using to distract me from the pain, I felt like a layer of my skin had been peeled away, leaving me raw.

I was grateful for having successfully put down the wine bottle, but I had to replace it with something healthy.

I decided to explore any tool available. I read every book I could, listened to podcasts, journaled and tried alternative healing methods like tapping (EFT) and EMDR. Some helped, some didn't, but the key is to treat your healing journey like a buffet. Take a little bit of everything, get seconds of what you like!

Some days were harder than others. A disturbing news story would cause panic attacks. I'd pace the floor for hours and call my therapist to tell her I couldn't breathe and felt like I was going to die. Some days the anxiety would get so bad I would scratch myself until I bled.

But the next day, I would get up and recommit to my one goal...taking back my life.

3. Change the tape.

When the horrible memory of my uncle surfaced, it magnified the chatter in my head to a deafening octave.

"You're damaged goods."

"No one will love you for you."

"These emotions are unbearable."

"I cannot survive this."

Maybe the internal messages are different, but we all have them.

"I'm a terrible mother for working so much."

"I'm a bad daughter for not visiting my parents more."

"I'm old and fat."

Or the one I hear the most from the women I mentor: "I'm not strong enough for this."

It's time to change the tape!

The words you're hearing are coming from your own mind of which you are the director.

Forget who you've been or who you thought you were. Who do you want to become?

When I meet with women who've experienced similar trauma, we talk about the fact that what happened to us is in the past. We practice taking deep breaths and being present, as it's in the present moment that we are safe. We are whole. We are strong. And we are no longer victims.

As we begin to release the hold our memories have on us, a beautiful space opens. One of my group members discovered she was not just a survivor, but a gifted artist. Another became an herbalist. The innate talents that come forth when you give them space will astonish you!

As you give yourself permission to be all that you want to be, you'll engage with life in a whole new way.

And one day, as you're absorbed in what you love, it will suddenly occur to you, your abusive voice has gone quiet.

4. Forgive.

My parents were amazing people. They were loving and supportive my whole life, which made it difficult to process that they likely knew what was happening to me and did nothing to stop it.

After ten years of therapy, I confronted them. My father hung his head in shame. My mother denied that it happened.

Their reaction sliced open every wound I'd worked to heal.

I decided to get curious about my mother's reaction and after talking to some family members, concluded that there were many family secrets; secrets far too shameful for discussion. I often wondered if my mom and aunts suffered the same fate I had at the hands of their brother, my uncle. No one is talking so I'll never know. Not in this lifetime. And for today, that's ok.

Forgiveness became a lifeline for me and an act of self-preservation. I realized that holding onto anger would only anchor me to my past. Embracing forgiveness, I discovered, was a gift I gave myself. I put down any expectation I had, accepting the fact that apologies and repentance were not the answer.

The answer was to abandon my need for them. By letting go, I freed myself to find peace.

That freedom came from going inside myself. I found a light and a strength I never knew I had. Call it God, Higher Power, Divine Spirit, Mother Nature—whatever works for you—but I guarantee if you spend time nurturing that beautiful energy that lies deep inside you, something miraculous will take place. I know it did for me. I began to see that people like my pedophile uncle are sick. I don't have to take on their illness or their journey. I have my own place on this earth and my own journey; one that allows me to explore joy, love, forgiveness and most of all, service to others to help them heal as I have.

REMEMBERING MY OWN POWER

This journey began with the resurfacing of a painful memory but healed through the cultivation of a powerful truth.

You see, through healing, I finally remembered my own authority. I remembered that as a human being, I have the capacity to create, and recreate, my own life. I have the innate ability to heal and regenerate as many times as it takes.

And so do you!

When I finally started telling my story, a few things became clear.

One, the more willing we are to share our experience, the more lives we can help and change.

Two, healing is not a phase or season, but an ongoing way of life that is both demanding and worth it.

And three, surviving and healing from trauma in no way impacted my ability to build a wildly successful career and in fact, helped me build even better relationships with my family, friends, colleagues and clients.

I have a life beyond my wildest dreams today.

Regardless of where you've been and where you might be now, you can still shoot for the stars, and I hope you do.

Because the next woman might be watching. Pull yourself through the darkness. Stand as a symbol of transformation and resilience.

Every moment you commit to choosing the light, you're not just helping yourself; you're showing someone else that life after trauma is possible, beautiful, and absolutely worth fighting for.

About Helene

Helene has been providing strategic marketing communications, advertising, public relations and digital marketing consulting services to her clients for more than twenty-five years. During that time, she has worked with numerous Fortune 500 companies as well as start-ups in various industries including Fintech, Health Care, Government and Manufacturing.

Helene is a born storyteller. She most likely adopted that skill from her grandfather, Henry Clay, who by all family member accounts was a wonderful, kind and gentle man who could 'spin a yarn' better than anyone. Perhaps that's why Helene was destined to become an expert PR practitioner, her profession often referred to as "spin doctors."

Her philosophy has always been to jump in with both feet and completely dedicate her time and efforts to achieving her client's business and marketing objectives. Her unwavering commitment to her clients has paid off. After working both on the corporate and agency side of the business, she launched her own PR/ad company and has been going strong since. She knows how to navigate economic swings and a COVID worldwide shutdown, and still maintains a profitable business. She is trained in AI strategies for business through an MIT learning program.

Some of Helene's personal accomplishments include two-time Boston Marathon runner; mini-triathlon and martial artist, achieving her first-degree Black Belt in Shaolin Kempo Karate.

Her passion for travel has taken her to just about every corner of the globe from the pyramids in Egypt, exquisite beaches in Sydney, city center of Auckland, New Zealand, warm waters of Maui, jungles of Malaysia, border of Nicaragua, salt baths in Costa Rica, red light district of Bangkok, horseback riding in the Canadian Rockies, and visiting her relatives on the Peloponnesian Island in Greece, to name a few.

Most important to her are the virtues her beloved Naval Commander father instilled in her; honor, integrity, honesty, generosity and hard work – all of which have served her well throughout her life. Her goal – help woman of all walks truly see their amazing potential and use it to love themselves as she has learned throughout her life.

Helene can be reached at helene@clay-comm.com, or visit her website at www.clay-comm.com.

CHAPTER 11

I KNOW THAT I KNOW THAT I KNOW

By Karen Petry

This wasn't supposed to happen.

I sat in my house, trying to make sense of the whirlwind of events I had been through.

This was not how it was supposed to go, and yet this was how it went. My heart ached as the full impact of the stress and loss finally hit me, and my mind presented a thousand different theories as to how I ended up here.

Perhaps I made a wrong turn or misunderstood God's direction.

Or perhaps all this time, I had been dreaming the wrong dream.

Now of course, I know that none of that was true. It's just that success is not a linear journey but a wild river. It twists and turns and its currents are unpredictable. One moment it glides smoothly in an intentional direction, and the next it crashes against boulders. Its waters are calm one day and a raging current the next.

Sometimes it looks totally stagnant, but the truth is, it's always in motion, always moving forward. The river's end cannot be seen, but is always there, always waiting.

What most people don't realize is that rivers often start at an elevated point, flow downhill as streams, pick up more water, eventually forming the large rivers that flow into the ocean.

It's up, it's down, it gains momentum, it stalls and flows again, and eventually, without fail, it reaches its destination. I am the river!

I was born in the south of Brazil. I was raised by loving parents, but we were very poor. As much as I loved my family and our small town, I knew there was more for me and that I was meant to travel the world. It wasn't just that I wished for it. I *knew* from the depths of my soul that I was meant to live a different, more abundant life outside that village.

My dream was to travel, get a good college education, and find a wonderful man to build an amazing family with.

And I did it! I lived in Europe and then moved to the United States.

I studied in reputable universities, received my bachelor's degree in communication and business, and then finished my master's degree in strategic brand communication.

I worked for major global corporations, received promotions and raises, and held important titles.

Then at last, I got married.

I thought, "Yes! I'm finally living my dream!"

And that's when the river crashed into the rocks.

My husband left me within weeks of getting married. COVID hit. My parents got very sick and so did I. I couldn't focus on work and at the age of thirty-six my dream life was completely gone.

I became confused, depressed, and angry.

Yet deep in my heart I still knew I was meant for abundance, love, and a family. Every bit of evidence was pointing to the exact opposite of that, but I knew that I knew that I knew.

Over a year later, I felt like my soul was finally healing and that's when I met my boyfriend, an extraordinary man who is patient and kind and loves me for who I am.

With him I gained an instant family, as he has two boys, and for the very first time I am called Mom.

I'm also a mom in waiting, as we prepare to adopt a group of siblings. The river has carried me to the exact destiny I dreamed of, this moment.

What about you? Is there a dream in your heart that's taking too long to materialize? Do you find yourself questioning if perhaps your inner knowing has been wrong all along?

I promise you it hasn't. There's a difference between a desire and a knowing. At the intersection of that difference is something we aren't all born with but we can learn to cultivate: confidence!

THE POWER OF CONFIDENCE

Confidence is not a mere feeling. It's not an act, a front, or a facade. It's a belief system built from within. Confidence is knowing that despite challenging circumstances, you know who you are and where you're heading.

You may not know every detail of the trajectory ahead, but the most important thing to remember is that confidence doesn't come from external sources or wins. In fact, you need to rely on confidence the most when you are repeatedly losing!

You will recognize a knowing because it is so strong and powerful that it becomes an unstoppable force of nature.

Such a knowing is the propeller force behind your most authentic self, and it has the power to overwrite any opinion, fear or circumstance.

To believe in your most authentic self is to have the confidence to transform your present life so it aligns with your vision. It's the difference between wishing you had something and *knowing* with conviction that it is already yours.

Dr. Nido Qubein, a wonderful speaker and president of High Point University once said there are no unrealistic dreams, only unrealistic timelines. So before you give up or question your own intuition, your faith, and your life, work on building your confidence muscle.

There are seven ways to build authentic confidence. These seven practices are how you build your resilience, keep your faith and ultimately manifest all that you know that you know that you *know*.

1. Fail big.

Give yourself permission to fail.

Often we focus so much on success that we forget that failure is an element of it.

We are taught to feel ashamed of our failures, making success the simple avoidance of failure. There's a saying that cemeteries are filled with wasted potential. People are so afraid to fail that they take their greatest talents to the grave, robbing the world of experiencing their brilliance.

So, what if you fail?

What's the big deal?

If you live your truth without the fear of failing, you allow these so-called failures to refine your vision and redirect your steps. In return, you embrace your failures as a learning curve that ultimately leads into your vision.

When you allow yourself to fail big, you're allowing the ebbs and flows to shape your authentic self.

True confidence is built upon authenticity and repetition.

Think of a baby learning to walk. They fall, they get up.

The more times you fall, the more times you get up.

That's how confidence is built.

The next time you fail, embrace the lesson with gratitude; for failures *always* precede success.

2. Stop comparing yourself.

Have you heard the saying that comparison is the thief of all joy? It's also the thief of dreams.

Comparing yourself to others is just as limiting as putting yourself in a box that's too small for you because it was designed for someone else.

Every time you compare yourself, you limit yourself. That isn't to say you shouldn't be inspired by others, but here's what we do:

We scroll social media and see that someone bought a nice house. We start comparing and feeling bad, and suddenly our focus is on manifesting a house like theirs. But what if the house you're meant to be in is much bigger and more beautiful than theirs?

You can look to your heroes and emulate their path, but ultimately, it's your own dreams that need your focus. When you compare yourself to others, you've taken your eyes off the road!

Your purpose and vision might be different than theirs.

And the destiny that's meant for you might be brighter and more beautiful than you, or they, could ever imagine.

3. Keep your promises.

If you want to build true confidence, following through on your commitments is imperative.

To build authentic confidence you need to know that your word matters, that you are trustworthy, starting with yourself.

Every year in January people make new year's resolutions.

Studies have shown that only 9% of people who make resolutions complete them!

If you make a commitment to yourself and don't follow through, more promises throughout the year will be made and broken because of the pattern established earlier in the year.

Why?

Once you allow yourself to break an important promise, it creates precedence for you to make more exceptions.

Only make promises you know you can keep. One of the keys to confidence is forming the belief that you, yourself are a safe bet.

By keeping your promises, you create a track record that builds on authentic confidence.

4. Stop trying; start doing.

How often have you heard somebody say, "Well, I'll try."

Words have power.

Every time you tell yourself, "I'll try," what you're telling yourself is that you will test it first to see if you like it or not.

Confident people don't try, they *decide*. They decide on a direction and continue to take action that moves them forward.

To try is essentially to give yourself an out!

That's ok if you're still trying to figure out your likes and dislikes in life, but think of it this way; would you elect a president who claims they will "try" to get the job done? Would you want a doctor performing surgery on you to say they will "try" to do it right?

We expect people to go beyond trying and fully commit.

The same applies to you. In 1519 the Spanish explorer Hernan

Cortéz, reached the shores of Mexico with his men and immediately told them to burn the ships. He wanted to remove any escape route. Burning the ships meant that they had to fully commit to their mission. There was no going back. They had to bet on themselves.

Otherwise, your commitment is vague, and the universe will respond in kind. It's like moving to a new country but having a return ticket.

Or moving in with your partner but keeping your own place.

If you want to build authentic confidence, you need to stop trying and start doing the things you set yourself to do. You are the CEO of your own life and that means you hold the most powerful position in your life.

Will you try, or will you *do*?

Answering that question is the difference between wishing for the life you want and having it!

5. Practice gratitude.

Confidence and scarcity cannot live in the same place. If you know you're meant for more, you must feel that abundance now! It's like having a closet full of money. If the door is closed, you can't see it, but you know it's there.

As you practice gratitude, you're giving thanks for all that you have and all that is yours, past, present, and future.

If life is too hard at this moment, how about being grateful for the air you breathe?

One of my best friends taught me this lesson. She's a strong mother to two beautiful girls. For several years she stayed in an abusive marriage to be part of her kids' lives, full time. Because she didn't want to put her kids through custody battles, she endured a horribly abusive relationship, until her husband finally let her and the kids go, amicably. Throughout her journey, we'd spend hours on the phone sharing stories while focusing on our dreams and working on vision boards. We'd praise God and give thanks in advance for our blessings as if we were already experiencing them. She'd say, 'Karen, I give thanks to God for I am alive. I thank God for breathing air into my lungs and for giving me another day to spend with my kids and serve others.' That's when I learned the true meaning of gratitude. If it feels like you have nothing to be grateful for, be thankful that you are still alive.

Be grateful for any overflow you have, and if you don't have much, be grateful for the blessing of *knowing—knowing that you are enough, that you are strong, and that you were uniquely created to be a blessing in this world.*

When an inner knowing is placed in your heart, consider it a fully funded mission from God. It's going to happen. You *know* that. Be grateful for its impending arrival.

6. Serve others—always.

> "Humility is not thinking less of yourself; it is thinking of yourself less. Humility is thinking more of others."
>
> —C. S. Lewis

That's great advice!

Serving others is a powerful catalyst for manifestation. When we focus our attention on those in need, we align our intentions with a Universal frequency of giving and receiving. The act of service generates a ripple effect, amplifying positive energy and drawing abundance into our lives.

Each gesture of kindness releases feel-good hormones like dopamine and the rush of that chemical leads to motivation and a reinforcement of your own aspirations. In uplifting others, we elevate ourselves, and the Universe responds to the vibrations, turning the seeds of our good deeds into the fruits of our reality.

7. Embrace change.

This might be the toughest one! Humans are naturally resistant to change. We crave familiarity and often when change occurs, we fight against it. It's exhausting to push against the current rather than flowing with it, yet that's what most of us do.

It's important to remember that change is a privilege only the living enjoy. If you are not changing, you're dead!

Be adaptable. Trust that every change thrust at you is a gift.

Change is sent to test your confidence. If you're merely wishing for something, a sudden change will spiral, but if you KNOW what's meant for you and hold an unwavering faith in its arrival, change is nothing more than a detour, or shortcut, to exactly where you need to go.

Trust that every change that comes your way, wanted or not, is a breadcrumb leading you closer to your dreams. It's not your job to tell God or the Universe when and how your dreams will be fulfilled. Your only job is to have unwavering confidence that they will come true.

The Untouchable Dream

Sometimes we have a dream that after a while seems impossible.

We get confused, discouraged, and angry.

We don't necessarily want to give up, but after so many years of setbacks and challenges, how do we know if we should continue to pursue it or not?

Because you'll know that you know that you know.

It won't be something that anyone can talk you out of. Despite all the evidence pointing to the contrary, your soul will hold a deep resonance with your dream that cannot be fractured. It's like an eternal flame. During the most challenging times, your knowing may dim, but it cannot be extinguished.

Trust in the light of your deepest desires and most compelling dreams. They are not fantasies, but seeds of truth planted in your heart. They are there because they are *yours*.

Hold them tight, have faith in their arrival and know that you know that you know that as you're reading this, those dreams are moving through the universe, weaving through time and making their way to your doorstep.

About Karen

For over two decades, Karen Petry has thrived as a communication expert, achieving success as a business strategist and program manager at two global corporations: Red Hat/IBM (a Fortune 500 company) and SAS (recognized as one of *Forbes'* America's Best Employers). Karen's passion for effective communication and leadership drove her to earn a bachelor's degree in communication and business, followed by a master's in strategic brand communication. Her expertise helps individuals and organizations communicate with purpose, strategy, and confidence.

As a communication strategist, Karen has empowered people from all over the world to align their goals with their deepest values. Her journey, from modest beginnings in southern Brazil to becoming an international communication expert, exemplifies the power of resilience and strategic thinking. At just eighteen, Karen embarked on her journey abroad, and today, with over twenty years' experience, she uses her background in strategic communication to help others build confidence and communicate effectively.

In her corporate career, Karen has successfully established new departments, expanded brand reach, boosted global revenue, streamlined processes, and fostered cohesive, high-performing teams. In 2020 she launched Vida by Design, a venture dedicated to helping men and women build confidence and design successful, fulfilling lives. Through Vida by Design, Karen has guided countless individuals to overcome doubts and insecurities, allowing them to rediscover their passions and realize their dreams—whether in business, relationships, or personal pursuits.

Karen's commitment to fostering personal growth extends beyond the professional world. She is a dedicated advocate for foster children and is preparing to adopt a group of siblings, driven by her deep compassion and belief in creating strong family bonds. In her free time Karen enjoys long beach walks with her boyfriend, Michael, and spending quality time with her family and her pug, Olive.

To connect with Karen, feel free to email her at karen@vidabydesign.com.

CHAPTER 12

AWAKENING THE PEACEMAKER WITHIN

By Barbara Chambliss

The planet does not need more successful people. The planet desperately needs more peacemakers, healers, restorers, storytellers, and lovers of all kinds.
—HIS HOLINESS THE DALAI LAMA

I t was a bright blue sky overhead as we stood on the dock of the island Krk off the coast of Croatia. We scanned the horizon for signs of the boat that was soon to arrive with nearly eighty children who had barely survived the Bosnian War.

The four prior war years had been full of betrayal for these children. The urban kids from Sarajevo never knew when the windows of their apartment building would blow out, never knew if their parent who darted from the cover of one demolished car to the next while fetching water or food would return alive, never knew when news would come that their best friend had become the victim of a land mine, never knew if it was their trusted uncle that revealed the family's hiding place to the enemy.

The rural kids from Srebrenica never suspected the enemy soldiers would defy the UN peacekeepers, march into their village and eliminate every male over age fourteen, killing them in front of their family or in a nearby mass grave. One little girl's hair had grown so long it hung past her knees, but she refused to cut it. It was the last thing her brother touched before the enemy soldiers killed him.

This camp was the brainchild of Judith Jenya. She had recruited us to be volunteer counselors at this camp. The sole purpose of the camp, she said, was to provide safe haven for these children. Safe meant predictable, trustworthy, a place where their nervous systems could calm down, where they could trust the adults, where they could just be kids.

Judith gave us two mandates: Never promise them something you don't deliver. And, much as we might be tempted, we weren't allowed to take any of them home with us.

We swam twice a day in the calming waters of the Adriatic. We hiked, played soccer, and sang songs together. We wrote our wishes in a bottle and threw it out to sea and every night had a disco dance.

Day by day, with patience and time, the children began to trust us. Beds were no longer wet, hair twirling ceased, talents emerged, teenagers from different religions fell in love. These children who had seen the very worst of humanity found fragments of joy in life's simplicity. And as they did, our hearts broke open.

When it was time to go home, the children begged us to come and see the physical damage the war had done. They wanted us to tell the world what we saw. They believed the world was unaware, because if the world knew about it, surely, they would've never let this war last four years.

As we arrived in Sarajevo, we watched the pain return to their eyes. Their homes, schools, and hospitals had been destroyed. Their bikes were demolished; their pets had died of starvation.

The national library was devastated by grenades, every book and piece of art burned including the documents that recorded rich Balkan history.

Throughout the country, bridges were blown up, mosques were obliterated, towns were bulging with displaced families.

When I saw these conditions, I was overcome with emotion.

On the plane ride home, my heart ached. I'd gone to Croatia to collect stories for my PhD dissertation, but I knew this was no longer an academic endeavor. I'd been transformed. I'd been given a once in a lifetime opportunity to witness and combat the ugliness of violence.

My purpose stood before me in crystal clarity. My purpose was now to wake up the conscious active peacemaker in myself and in as many people as possible.

My PhD dissertation was titled "Women Peacemakers: The Hidden Side of Peacemaking." I personally interviewed women in Europe, Asia, South America and the U.S. This ignited three more decades of interviewing over 60 ordinary women doing extraordinary acts of peacemaking throughout the world. I recently published a book with fifteen of their stories entitled *Women Peacemakers: What We Can Learn from Them.*

This year, on my eightieth birthday, I opened my desk drawer and found the recordings of forty-five interviews not yet published. I made up my mind that day.

I would not die with those stories in the drawer. I would keep sharing them with the world. And I would keep helping people wake up to the peacemaker within.

WHAT IS THIS KIND OF PEACEMAKING?

It begins with noticing something unequal, unjust, or unfair. Then, with permission, the peacemaker works *alongside* the underprivileged to help them gain the skills needed to rise to a position of equal opportunity, equal empowerment, and equal respect.

People often mistakenly associate the term peacemaker with grand gestures, large-scale initiatives, or volunteering for high-profile organizations.

While large-scale efforts are important, the cumulative effect of everyday actions by ordinary people is what ultimately changes the world.

For my PhD I decided to interview ordinary women doing extraordinary acts of peacemaking. If, that is, I could get them to see that they were indeed peacemakers.

The PhD Committee required that every woman had to be

recommended by two sources: someone else and themselves. I would soon learn that women often don't see themselves for the heroines they are. Most of the time, when they performed their highest acts of peacemaking, they weren't moved by heroism, but humanity. That's why this work often goes unrecognized as peacemaking.

That's how it happened for Connie Ning. Connie's peacemaking was sparked when she looked into the eyes of a woman in postwar Vietnam dying of cancer and with no medicine to ease her pain. Connie was dumbfounded that there were still places where people had to die in pain simply due to lack of access. She returned home to Colorado, collected unused medical supplies and sent them to Vietnam, eventually founding the Friendship Bridge, an organization that provided educational and economic opportunities to women and children in both Vietnam and Guatemala.

When I interviewed Connie, I was surprised to hear her say that she had a cofounder. She explained that her cofounder was the woman whose death inspired her work.

"If she hadn't looked in my eyes before she died," Connie said, "there would be no Friendship Bridge."

"Ah," I thought to myself, "that's true, but also, there would be no Friendship Bridge if the window to Connie's soul hadn't opened that day and revealed her potential to change the world."

HOW TO BE A PROACTIVE, CONSCIOUS PEACEMAKER FOR OTHERS—AND FOR *YOURSELF*

I can relate to the resistance of accepting such a noble title. After my trip to work with Bosnian War victims, a local paper published a story with a headline that read "Local peacemaker goes to Croatia."

I was uncomfortable! I didn't see myself in any kind of exalted light. I was just a woman who had said yes to an opportunity to comfort children whose hearts had been broken.

I realized that often our first acts of peacemaking are

spontaneous. We fall into them, jarred by a shocking discovery. Once there, thrust into a scene of heartache our souls can't shake, our role as peacemaker shifts from spontaneous to ongoing daily conscious commitment.

Sometimes it happens when we become aware of the plight of a marginalized group or witness an act of prejudice. And sometimes our inner warrior is awakened when it finally occurs to us that the victim of injustice is ourselves.

However our journey unfolds, there are elements of peacemaking that are universally shared by those who answer the call. There are many, but if you find yourself drawn to peace, start with these three lessons from the women peacemakers, and commit every day to consciously choosing them as your compass.

1. Be awake when the opportunity arises.

Such was the situation for Somboon Srikhamdokhae.

While working in the spinning and ironing room of a large cotton textile factory in Thailand, Somboon lost 52% of her lung capacity from the cotton fibers in her work environment. She wasn't looking to step into a peacemaker's role, but once she looked *at* it, she couldn't look away.

As the first person to sue a Bangkok employer for inadequate safety conditions in the workplace, Somboon led 350 workers in a class action suit, which held employers responsible, including reparations for the damages sustained by the workers.

She created a self-help network for people afflicted with occupational illnesses which acted as a lobbying group to draw attention to issues that had been taboo in Thailand.

Imagine how many people would have continued to tolerate toxic conditions if Somboon hadn't found the courage to take a stand.

While her own health was the match that lit the spark, it was the drive to save others that shifted the tides of working conditions in Thailand.

But you don't have to lead a movement to be a peacemaker. When you see something, *do* something. It can be as simple as helping someone carry their groceries or standing up for a stranger being bullied. Or, with a daily commitment, over time you may find you have quietly helped a whole body of people lift themselves up, like Somboon did.

It can also be a courageous act of *self*-focused justice.

Once you awaken to knowing you are suffering an injustice, that your soul is being insulted or your self-worth endangered, do not go back to sleep.

Stay awake. Be vigilant in the protection of your boundaries. Stay focused on achieving your own inner peace.

2. Develop your service in response to an expressed need.

There's a saying that encourages us to treat others how we want to be treated.

I invite you, instead, to treat others how *they* want to be treated.

Anytime we feel called to help another, it's important that we listen to their needs rather than acting on our own preconceived notions.

Often, our assumptions don't align with their reality. Imagine that a local charity works to serve a community facing food insecurity. They might assume that the best way to help is to provide people with pre-packaged meals they can pop into the microwave. Had they listened, however, they would've learned that most of the people didn't have a microwave and were in desperate need of access to a community kitchen.

When we take the time to get curious about the needs of others, we can provide support that is both meaningful *and* effective.

3. Work *with* not *for*.

One day my phone rang and set in motion an entirely new branch of my purpose.

A mother of a middle-school student was struggling with her daughter who was part of a friend group that had turned toxic, and she asked if I would help.

I did, and soon the principal called and asked if I would work with the entire school.

We trained two mediators in every classroom. We taught the whole student body the language of peace-making and then taught the same skills to teachers, administrators, lunch ladies and bus drivers.

It was so successful that we expanded the program to many schools in Colorado and, surprisingly, one in Israel.

I also teach high school students the skills of Proactive Conscious Peacemaking I learned from the women I interviewed. After reading the women's stories from the book, the students devise an act of peacemaking of their own.

One high school group interviewed sixteen elderly people who felt unnoticed in their community. They videoed the conversations and showed them at the local theater to a packed house!

Another group chose to learn mediation skills and teach the skills to the third- and fourth-graders in their school. The result was that the school now had thirty mediators in their building!

Can you imagine the extraordinary ripple effect that just those two events had on the community?

When you work *with* people, rather than *for* them, and encourage them to take part in building their own empowerment, you are delivering one of the highest forms of respect—acknowledging their potential to leave an indelible mark on the world.

WHEN THE PEACE YOU NEED TO MAKE IS WITH YOURSELF

As a result of some trauma in my life, I've struggled with feelings of inadequacy. I tried to overcome that by pushing myself. I got a bachelor's degree, three master's degrees, and a PhD. Still, I questioned my own worth.

I began to work with people who suffered trauma and found that often trauma victims try hard to deny or overcome their memories when the most effective thing they can do is work *through* them.

It's true for any kind of trauma. Whether you grew up in

dysfunction or married into it, pain is pain. How then do we stay in peace without turning into a silent doormat or a raging lion?

You take a breath, and ask yourself these questions:

What do I need to feel safe?

What would feel the most like self-respect?

Listen to and heed the answer.

You might be guided to leave, or to spend an afternoon outside, or write a letter to the person who hurt you.

Whatever answer comes, it's coming from the depths of your soul. Heed its wisdom.

Because while I've found that one of the best ways to heal ourselves is to help others, and you cannot be truly available for others, until you have healed yourself.

WALKING, AND PAVING, THE PATH TO PEACE

I'm a fourth-generation Coloradan. I'd rather sleep under the stars than beneath a roof and feel intricately connected to the magic of the Rocky Mountains. For fun I sing cowboy songs in a Cowboy Corral. Out of respect for victims of gun violence, we decided to stop performing any songs that mention a gun.

Yet a gun is neutral, nothing more than a hunk of metal. It's when we add bullets, emotions, and intentions to guns that they become weapons of destruction. This is one trait that violence and peacemaking share—they both begin with *intention.*

When you have a choice, get conscious. If you *intend* to be curious and genuinely listen, you are headed toward peace. If you *intend* to be critical and retributive, you are headed toward violence. Aim for collaboration over competition. Forge mutual respect. Choose wisely—every time.

Being a catalyst for peace is not rocket science. Anyone of any age can set the intention to act in the face of injustice.

Every one of us can begin by becoming curious, listening intently to others, and allowing ourselves to be moved and inspired.

You don't have to move mountains or become a household

name. Sometimes the quietest acts of courage and service have the most far-reaching impact.

For to stand in the mantle of the peacemaker is simply to stand in the mantle of a caring human being, with all the dynamic and glorious potential we hold within.

About Barbara

Barbe Chambliss is a psychotherapist, a mediator, and an organic farmer. She's had a lifelong interest in how peace is made. Professionally she directed the Volunteer Center for Conflict Resolution in Aspen, Colorado. She has taught mediation skills to over five hundred children and adults in rural Colorado. She facilitates Restorative Justice Circles in her community. Shortly after the terrorist attacks on New York City, she compiled and distributed a "Working Compendium of Non-violent Responses to 9/11." She later served as a therapist on a US military base to better understand the human dynamics of converting citizens to soldiers.

For her PhD dissertation, titled "Women Peacemakers: The Hidden Side of Peacemaking," Barbe personally interviewed little-known women in Europe, Asia, South America, and the US who were doing extraordinary acts of peacemaking. This ignited three more decades of interviewing over sixty ordinary women doing extraordinary acts of peacemaking throughout the world. She recently published a book with the stories of fifteen of these women, titled *Women Peacemakers: What We Can Learn from Them*.

Halfway through this journey Barbe volunteered as a counselor in a Croatian camp providing a safe haven for eighty children who had barely survived the Bosnian War. This changed everything for her. She came home with the committed purpose of waking up the peacemaker in herself and as many people as possible. She now teaches Proactive Conscious Peacemaking to high school students and adults.

Barbe is a fourth-generation Coloradan and the mother of three children and six stepchildren. She'd rather sleep under the stars than beneath a roof and revels in being outdoors in all seasons of her beloved Rocky Mountains. She recharges her soul by spending time at a cabin perched on the edge of an alpine meadow she shares with a herd of elk and a chorus of coyotes. For fun she sings and yodels in a Cowboy Corral.

Learn more about her at www.barbechamblissauthor.com.

CHAPTER 13

FAITH IS YOUR MOST POWERFUL COPILOT

By Latonia Wallace Copeland

When a plane malfunctions, the atmosphere shifts from routine to urgent in an instant.

At the sound of alarms and the flash of warning lights, the crew kicks into crisis mode, drawing on a blend of training and instinct to identify and mitigate the issue before a minor malfunction becomes a catastrophe.

The airplane's technology is designed for this type of unforeseen circumstance, and the pilot knows how to execute emergency protocols, read any data coming through, and make critical decisions under urgent pressure.

It's a delicate balance of human knowledge and technical preciseness relying on one another to bring everyone on board to safety.

If the pilot can keep cool and keenly focus on their many skills, the result is often a successful landing.

But if the pilot panics and freaks out, the odds may be despairingly different.

I've worked in the aviation industry in various roles for nearly twenty-five years.

During that time, my life has repeatedly felt like an airplane on the brink of malfunction. Perhaps you can relate. You're humming along, falling in love, raising kids, going to work, and *yikes*! Mechanical failure.

The malfunction can come in the form of a loss, a divorce, a diagnosis or a termination of employment. For me it was all those things, multiple times.

At that point we have a choice—to shut down and crash, or to heal, realign, and restore our aircraft to smooth sailing and a safe landing.

When Crisis Strikes

There are four steps to mitigating an aircraft crisis:

1. Fly the aircraft. In the case of a crisis, the first thing to do is maintain control of the plane. Don't panic; focus on keeping the aircraft flying.

2. Find the best glide speed. Adjust the aircraft to its best glide speed. This speed varies depending on the specific aircraft model and weight.

3. Trim the aircraft. Adjust the balance to maintain a desired altitude or flight path and reduce the output and workload.

4. Identify the issue later. Don't worry about diagnosing the problem immediately. Just stick to crisis mitigation.

Fly the aircraft.

Over a fourteen-month period I experienced a divorce, bankruptcy, two job losses, and a short sale of my home, all in short succession.

The divorce was not a shock. My husband and I had gone through years of painful ups and downs. Eventually this affected my health and wellbeing. Divorce always comes with a side of deep disappointment and sometimes regret.

At the same time, while I was navigating a new normal as a single mother, the airline I was working for folded. I was quickly able to secure a job at another airline and felt that perhaps my luck was finally changing.

I was wrong!

One morning, as I was getting ready for work, my babysitter called and said, "Turn on your television. A plane just went through the World Trade Center."

I walked into the family room where the kids were watching cartoons and changed the channel. We watched as the second plane hit the second tower. I broke down in tears, not just because it was clear that we were watching history being altered, but because the news was reporting the closing of all airports, and I knew that my job was in jeopardy. I soon learned that many lives were lost. The stress escalated.

I had three children to feed, a dog, three cars, and a mortgage I could barely afford.

For days, airline employees were in limbo, and within a week, the airline I worked for shut down for good.

I had to quickly make very tough decisions during that period. I did a short sale on my home and moved my family to a much smaller apartment. I had to get rid of many of my belongings, rehome our dog, and start completely over.

Life happens like that sometimes. With no rhyme or reason, we are hit with back-to-back trials, and we can panic and shut down, or we can breathe, maintain control and keep flying.

I decided that my children would not watch me crash! I was going to show them what perseverance looked like.

I had always wanted to work for Delta Air Lines. A colleague told me to visit the Delta Connection office and tell them she sent me. When I arrived, the receptionist asked if I had an appointment. I said, "No, but I was told to come here and ask for Mike."

She said that if I didn't have an appointment, I would be out of luck. I didn't know who Mike was at that point, but I wasn't leaving that building until I talked to him!

Eventually, Mike agreed to see me. He hired me on the spot, and I stayed with Delta's organization for twenty-two years.

But it wasn't all smooth sailing. In 2010 an unprecedented tsunami struck Japan. Delta cut approximately two hundred merit jobs, and I was offered a severance package. I declined it and changed positions, which required me to basically start all over…again. It made me realize that I could not have all my eggs in one basket.

I decided to start my own side business in 2014 and launched an event production company. I loved it and told myself that if another opportunity presented itself to retire from the airline industry, I would take it.

In 2020 that opportunity came knocking!

During COVID-19, I left Delta and became a full-time entrepreneur. I grew my event and travel business while working in ministry, serving as a Global Peace Ambassador to the UN, under Word of Life Ministries International.

Find the best glide speed.

In crisis mitigation, the goal is to find your best glide speed, and that's what I did.

Sometimes it takes a few tries to get it right.

Sometimes you've got to unexpectedly embrace a pivot to keep steady.

Sometimes you've got to abandon one plan and open your arms to another.

Gliding isn't something that happens by luck but by an unwavering determination to keep adjusting, keep trying, and stay more focused on the solutions than the problems.

When faith is all that's left

One of the unexpected things about being human is that most of us don't live our lives braced for impact, which means that when impact hits, it's a total shock.

Well, it shouldn't be. We know that life is full of twists and turns and light and darkness and yet that awareness does nothing to ease the jolt of pain that comes with loss.

2023 was one of the most difficult years I've had to overcome. In March, while visiting my eighty-year-old father, his already fragile health changed drastically. We spent a great day together, dining and at the nail shop.

The next day, he was sent to the emergency room, and during dialysis after hours of waiting, I was told he would need to transfer to a different hospital. During the transport, the ambulance carrying my father was in a horrific accident involving an 18-wheeler, three cars, and the ambulance. This day would drastically change my father's life and elevate his condition, as he was left paralyzed.

My siblings and I rotated our schedules to take turns visiting the hospital and caring for him. I flew back and forth to Arkansas from Atlanta frequently. One week, just as I had returned home, and just days after Mother's Day, I received a phone call.

"You need to come to the hospital," the nurse said. "Your nephew is here." My nephew lived nearby, and he had just texted me the day before the holiday.

When his mom and I arrived at the hospital, he was in critical condition. He died within a week, and to this day we don't know what happened to him.

Over the summer, I continued to fly back and forth to visit my dad, assisting with caring for him and my mom, who also lives in Arkansas, and maintain my event business.

In December, while setting up an event, my daughter called me in tears. Her father, my ex-husband, had died. I told my daughter to come to me; I held her close and then finished my event setup.

On December 30 we flew to Indiana for the funeral, and while I was there mourning the loss of my child's father, my own father passed away.

Trim the aircraft.

When a crisis strikes, it is vital to do everything you can to maintain a balance and limit the stress and output of the pilot.

For me the key to that balance is faith.

When I cannot find my way, when things spin out of control, when life seems to malfunction again and again, I turn to prayer.

I pray over myself, my loved ones and even my adversaries because I see everyone and everything as a manifestation of the spirit.

A lot of people have asked me how I maintain such a strong

faith in the face of so much loss, and here is my answer: Faith in God does not get you around trouble. It gets you *through* it.

There are times that more out*put* cannot change the out*come*.

In those moments, faith must drive.

Identify the issue later.

It's also a crucial time to lean in to step 4, which is to identify the problem later. When catastrophe strikes, agonizing over the cause of it not only wastes precious time, but it distracts you from the most important task at hand: healing.

If you can let go of your need to know *why*, trust God's plan and cultivate a belief that everything that happens is meant to grow you, and that every detour is directing you to the next level of strength, you'll find that you can keep going even in the most trying circumstances.

It's not easy. When life throws curve ball after curveball, it's human nature to deeply feel each blow. Our default setting is to come to a screeching halt and wonder, "Why me? Why this? Why now?"

But remember, stick to crisis mitigation, to breathing, and to healing.

Our fear will tell us to give up.

Our grief will tell us to shut down.

And that's why it's so important that we learn to listen to the most loud and important voice—the voice of the Spirit.

Because it is the only voice that speaks the truth.

Turn to Your Crew

When a plane takes off, it takes off against the wind, not with it.

And yet with power and determination it pushes through. Up it goes, continuing its climb against the wind's powerful force, never pulling back until it reaches safe cruising altitude.

Imagine if at the first sign of resistance the pilot just gave up.

For us resistance comes in the form of setbacks, failures, and obstacles that slow our progress and test our resolve.

One of the best antidotes to these challenges is a solid support system.

It sounds cliché, yet you'll find the concept of group support at the foundation of every recovery program, every religion, and every healing modality.

Just as a pilot depends on a copilot to share the responsibilities and provide a second set of eyes, we lean on our closest friends and family for guidance and assistance. The flight crew ensures that the passengers' needs are met and tended to, much like our social circle provides emotional support and assistance through life's ups and downs.

Meanwhile, God is like air traffic control, overseeing the broader picture and offering crucial navigation guidance to help us avoid or push through our most challenging scenarios.

The presence of a support system is vital to our health and well-being. Yet, their presence is useless if we don't learn to call on them in our moments of need.

A friend can only help if we ask for help.

A group can only benefit us if we show up to it.

And a higher power is always at work, we just need to tune into it.

Whatever your beliefs are around God, I like to think of it as a radio signal.

Call it what you want—God, the universe, a higher power, guardian angels—but much like the radio, the signal is always available. The songs are always playing, you just don't hear them until you make the decision to flip the radio on and turn the volume up!

Faith and support are the same. They require our action, our invitation and our willingness to receive. Only when we tune into love, support and spirit can we reap the blessings and miracles of Divine intervention.

Only when we remember our own God-gifted power can we work to restore our hearts.

Fasten Your Seatbelts

As I write this, I've just been to visit my husband, who has suffered a stroke.

Yes, it's painful, but I know now that it's just turbulence, and turbulence is to be expected.

Life ebbs and flows and the joy of love, laughter and peace is often followed by the pain of unexpected loss or a curve ball we never saw coming.

I have learned to embrace the ups and downs because after all, they are proof of life. If I am still navigating the highs and lows, I am still breathing.

Luckily, I also know that I've got the tools to turn to for help and healing and so do you.

Your faith is your oxygen mask, dropping down from the ceiling at the exact moment you need it.

Your friends and family are your floatation device, holding you afloat when you're hurting and carrying you safely to shore.

And the black box on every plane that holds all the data cannot be destroyed.

That's your spirit. It stands strong and unbreakable. It steels against rough skies. It pushes through unexpected storms.

And if you remember its power and resilience, it will always guide you to a safe landing, helping you touch down gently and holding you while you heal, until it's time, once again, to get up and fly.

About Latonia

Ambassador Latonia Wallace Copeland is a distinguished luxury and design expert, renowned for her passion for exemplary service in both business and life. With over twenty-five years' experience in consumer sales, event production, and design, she has established herself as an organic professional adept at infusing creative flair into any event. Latonia's extensive background in hospitality and aviation further enhances her ability to deliver high-quality service.

In May 2023, Latonia was honored as a Global Peace Ambassador to the United Nations under Word of Life Ministries International. She actively serves within the Women's Leadership group and the Children's International Affairs Department. Her dedication to community service is evident through her numerous volunteer projects in both the corporate and private sectors, earning her multiple accolades.

As the CEO of Essential Affairs, an event production and design company, Latonia is celebrated for her talent in tailoring ambiance to reflect the client's personality while achieving impressive results. She combines a love for luxurious templates, linens, and decor with inspirations drawn from nature, exotic flowers, and wisdom, bringing a unique flair to the event industry.

Latonia has a deep commitment to the success of communal youth. As a military spouse, mother, and sibling, she embodies a loving and caring spirit, dreaming of creating opportunities for youth entrepreneurship through creativity. She values higher education and has a proven history of achievement in applied sciences with a focus on graphic design and business management, along with certifications in various multidisciplinary skill sets.

Ambassador Copeland has achieved numerous accolades and held various prestigious roles throughout her career. She serves as a love and interfaith chaplain. Additionally, she is a board member of Pink STEM Engineering, an active member of the National Council of Negro Women, and a host of international organizations. Her past roles include serving as president of the CPO at MLK Jr. High School in Decatur, Georgia, a youth mentor for the Steve and Marjorie Harvey Foundation, and a Brand Ambassador for Lisa Cloud, founder of the Lisa Nicole Collection, and Millionaires.

141

Contact information:

Pinterest: @EssentialAffairsForYou
Instagram: @EssentialAffairs
Facebook: @LatoniaWallaceCopeland
LinkedIn: @LatoniaWallaceCopeland

Essential Affairs LLC
Email: info@essentialaffairsevents.com, latoniac604@gmail.com
Website: www.essentialaffairsevents.com

> Commit your work to the LORD, and your plans will be established.
> —PROVERBS 16:3 (ESV)

CHAPTER 14

TRUE SUCCESS

Aligning Actions with Authentic Desires

By Meg McSherry

The first sign of trouble is the check-engine light.

The red light catches your attention, and for a split second your thoughts divert from the endless to-do list in your head as you wonder what the light could be signaling.

But life is busy, so the light stays on day after day, desperately trying to warn you of impending malfunction, but eventually, it just becomes invisible.

Then, the rattle starts. You hear it as soon as you start driving, so you turn down the radio and listen intently, trying to figure out where the noise is coming from. Only your calendar is packed this week and work is crazy, so you assure yourself that it's nothing. Soon the rattle becomes louder and what made you turn down the radio to hear it, makes you turn up the radio to drown it out.

Occasionally, between meetings and grocery shopping the thought to get the car serviced crosses your mind but you press on, naively hoping everything will be ok.

And that's why, when your car comes to a total stop in the middle of a busy intersection, it's not the car you'll be swearing at but yourself!

We all do this.

Life does its job of delivering early warning signals that things are falling apart, and we do our very human job of ignoring them completely.

We don't mean to. It's just that we have things to do and warped definitions of success and soon, we're exhausted, paralyzed by anxiety and wondering how we'll ever climb out of the hole we dug for ourselves.

Or maybe that's just me…

It wasn't that long ago I ignored my own check engine light and ended up knee deep in total burnout.

I'm a business owner and was determined to grow my business to meet the needs of my community. For months I'd been working 12-hour days. I'd taken a risk when I made the decision to expand the business and my family was supportive, but I hadn't paid myself in months and the weight of this decision bore down on me like a refrigerator full of bricks.

I didn't want to let my family or my staff down, so as the reality hit that I may not be able to keep the doors open, I did what any smart business owner with an advanced degree would do…worked harder and longer to prevent it from happening.

Hopefully you sense the sarcasm in that statement as that was not the best call! Burnout consumed me, and anxiety crept in as I feared the possibility of becoming ill. What would happen then? What would happen if I was so burnt out that I became ill?

That's the funny thing about burnout, fear and anxiety. They are gateway emotions to just about every worst-case scenario your mind can dream up! For me, the fact that I had put myself in dire straits was doubly frustrating because I'm trained to get people *out* of them.

Right around that time, I participated in a one-day course on New Year's Day to jump start the year. During it, we were asked a series of questions to help us set goals.

I was totally paralyzed. I couldn't answer the questions. I couldn't define one thing to reach for because I couldn't see out of the deep hole I was in.

After that wake-up call, I did the most uncomfortable thing I could think of to do…I asked for help. In that moment, a weight lifted off my shoulders. It was time to break the pattern of thinking that my worth was tied to my business's success or failure.

This realization changed everything. With the support of my husband, friends and community, I refocused on what I truly wanted and needed and downsized my business.

Then, a funny thing happened. Nothing fell apart! In fact, as I aligned my actions with my genuine desires, I regained both time and financial freedom. True success didn't come from working harder in the wrong direction. It came from harmony, being surrounded by the right people and pursuing the passions closest to my heart.

Now I know it was time to become my own client and take my own advice, because it works! If you're struggling, if clarity eludes you, if exhaustion is setting in, here's what to do...

GET HONEST WITH YOURSELF

For the past several years, I've been helping people who suffer from anxiety, trauma, depression and grief.

Often by the time a client calls me, their check-engine light has been on for months. A lot of people think they're just exhausted or overworked and this assumption prevents them from reaching out for help sooner. What typically happens is that something in their life has changed or fallen out of resonance. They may have experienced a loss or some other struggle that paralyzes them from moving forward.

I like to ask when they first noticed something was off, and often it's clear their body was talking to them long before they decided to finally listen!

"I was exhausted."

"I felt numb."

"I was just so overwhelmed."

"My gut was telling me something was off."

All of these common answers are signals our bodies send to warn of impending breakdowns, and all of them are invitations to go deeper.

I was busy, overworked and exhausted when I was trying to

grow my business. Underneath that, however, was a deeper feeling—fear that if I slowed down, I would fail.

And underneath *that,* lived an even deeper fear that if I failed, I would let down the people I cared about.

I was leaving all these feelings unchecked, distracting myself with busyness when what I really needed to do was press pause, check in with my heart and listen to the messages my body and soul were sending.

Maybe you've been there? You agree to bake for the school because what if you say no and people talk about you?

You ignore the exhaustion you feel after spending time with your partner because you can't imagine having to navigate a breakup.

You quiet the anxiety you feel when the bills come in because budgeting feels totally overwhelming.

It's human nature to seek instant gratification and look for easy buttons, but when we leave feelings and warning signals unchecked, we're setting ourselves up for bigger problems down the road. You can't begin to heal what you haven't acknowledged. That's why the first step is the hardest one.

If you want to pull yourself up from the cliff, you've got to first admit that you're hanging from it.

RUFFLE THE FEATHERS AND ROCK THE BOATS

There's an epidemic going on and while anyone can fall victim to it, women are its favorite target. The symptoms are subtle. We say yes when we mean no. We ignore the signs of fatigue and other biological clues. We defer to the benchmarks of success set for us by others, and the social media feed that shows how well our friends or acquaintances are doing which of course, makes us question if we are doing well *enough.*

We take jobs and projects we don't want because the family needs the money. We accept invitations we aren't interested in to avoid being uncomfortable.

We keep the peace without ever stopping to question whose

peace we're keeping because our goal is to not ruffle any feathers or inconvenience someone else.

It's textbook people pleaser syndrome and too many of us are afflicted with it.

I grew up in a family of successful entrepreneurs and watched them work long, grueling hours. I thought I'd broken the unhealthy balance by choosing a 9–5 career, yet there I was, falling into the same hustle and grind rhythm. I realized I had tied my identity to how hard I was working and how much money was coming in.

For some reason, I didn't feel I could justify giving *myself* anything. I'd been conditioned by society to keep striving for more without ever stopping to ask if I wanted it and without measuring the deeper costs. I believed I was doing the right thing for everyone else and striving for what I thought would bring fulfillment.

The problem is that if we're living by other people's playbook, or basing our worth on not failing, we're out of integrity. It's only when we dare to live in alignment that we can claim authenticity.

Once you've become aware that you're not in a great place, the next step to pulling yourself out of misalignment is to take time to figure out what *you* really want. Not what you think you *should* want but what you deeply desire; how you would *really* spend your time if you weren't afraid of letting anyone down.

Author Glennon Doyle wrote, "Your job throughout your entire life, is to disappoint as many people as it takes to avoid disappointing yourself."

When I was working twelve-hour days, I convinced myself I was doing it in service to others. I was serving my family and my staff. The reality is that not one person in my life was feeling taken care of so long as I was *underserving* myself.

When I finally decided to downsize, my husband shocked me by saying, "I thought you should have done this a year ago!"

All that time I thought he wanted me to work hard, and I worried he'd be disappointed if I gave up. Can you relate? You engage in acts of self-abuse under false assumptions only to find out it was all for nothing!

The key to success is never hidden behind the door of self-abuse. So, ruffle the feathers, rock the boats, rattle every cage you can if it means you honor the voice of your intuition, the wisdom of your body and ultimately, the purpose you are here to live.

Move Toward Discomfort

When I decided to restructure my business, I knew that meant letting go of some staff. I had never laid anyone off before and it was tough.

I felt guilty but more than that, I felt like my values were in a tug of war. I needed to let people go, but my sense of duty and integrity were battling my sense of practicality.

How could a decision that was right for me *really* be right if it hurt other people?

But then it hit me. What if this integral part of *my* journey was also a catalyst for *theirs*?

What if, in being laid off, they found their next best thing? What if it allowed them the space and time to tune in to their own desires?

In the end I gave everyone as much notice as I could and handled it in the most empathetic way possible, but it was uncomfortable.

That's the thing no one tells you about growth and healing. The parts of it that are necessary are never comfortable. Remember what it felt like to be a teenager learning to drive? Or a first-time parent taking a newborn home from the hospital? None of that is comfortable, but we don't turn back. We move into the discomfort and in doing so, prove to ourselves that we can survive it.

If we ever want to do anything new or grow in any way, we've got to become comfortable in the discomfort.

Ultimately, I realized that growth often feels like a tightrope walk between fear and possibility. There is a sequence to discomfort. When you first enter it, you feel anxious. Then you do what needs to be done and you feel stronger. Finally, having made it through to the other side, you are gifted with a blend of relief and pride.

You've done it! And you can do it again.

FIND YOUR TRIBE

There is a reason that support and recovery programs operate in groups.

Human beings are wired for community. Healing is meant to be a team sport. When I was struggling, I reached out to my husband, my friends and my colleagues.

This is perhaps the most important piece of the healing pie! You've got to bring yourself out of isolation.

In my case, talking to people who had been through similar experiences helped me see things from a new perspective. They shared their struggles and triumphs and I realized I wasn't alone.

Think about the last time you faced a significant obstacle. Maybe it was a tough decision or a major life change. Odds are, you sought out the opinions of people you respect. Or perhaps, people jumped in to help without even being asked. Their support wasn't just a comfort, it empowered you to take the next step.

The next time you are struggling, resist the urge to isolate yourself. Instead, turn to your community. Fortified by their belief and the added armor of their wisdom, you'll find the courage and clarity you need to move forward.

According to a study by the American Society of Training and Development, people are 65 percent more likely to meet a goal after declaring their commitment to someone else. This increases to 95 percent if they have ongoing meetings with an accountability partner.

We are not meant to be alone. By joining with people we trust, we more easily take uncomfortable action toward overcoming our fear.

ACKNOWLEDGE YOUR FEELINGS, ESPECIALLY THE BAD ONES!

I originally thought my story was about navigating the space between burnout and recovery, but I realized it was more layered than that. Burnout was a symptom of a larger feeling left unchecked: fear.

I was afraid of working more, losing balance and getting sick.

I was afraid of downsizing and losing my income.

I was afraid that no matter what decision I made, I would disappoint someone.

Fear, left unchecked, is a formidable foe and wears many masks. It can transform into anxiety, exhaustion and even depression if ignored for too long.

A lot of people assume that the opposite of fear is courage, but I believe that the opposite of fear is *knowledge*.

I know that any anxiety I feel is fear, and that the antidote is to get curious about its origin. The more I logically dissect where the fear is coming from, the faster it loosens its grip.

When any negative feelings threaten to derail your life, consider this:

You can treat those feelings like enemies you *have* to conquer, or mysteries you *get* to solve.

I love a good mystery! Start by asking questions, embracing fears, and uncovering their origins. Notice any signs of misalignment early, like a warning light, and clarify what you want to fix before a minor issue becomes a major problem.

One thing that isn't a mystery any longer to me is the path to peace, healing, and happiness: Be in deep relationship with your own soul, learn to trust and follow your own intuition, reach out to others, and always, without fail, follow the truth of your own heart.

About Meg

Meg McSherry brings over twenty years of transformative experience in human development and mental health, establishing herself as a leading authority in anxiety management and personal growth. She has worked with renowned organizations such as the Department of Defense, the Department of Veterans Affairs, and various nonprofits, where her expertise has made a significant impact on improving the emotional health of those served by the organizations. As a successful entrepreneur, Meg continues to empower individuals and organizations, helping them achieve lasting change and growth.

Meg is passionate about supporting business leaders, C-level executives, and entrepreneurs who are navigating the complexities of managing leadership, personal satisfaction, and business growth. Her clients are successful individuals facing challenges such as decision-making under pressure, managing team dynamics, and sustaining a clear strategic vision in a rapidly changing market. Meg provides tailored coaching that addresses these unique challenges, offering solutions for stress management, conflict resolution, and enhancing emotional intelligence. By working with Meg, leaders gain clarity, resilience, and the skills needed to lead their organizations or businesses with confidence, ultimately achieving both professional and personal fulfillment.

Her journey began by assisting individuals in achieving remarkable recovery from trauma, igniting her passion to uncover lasting solutions for anxiety and life challenges. This pursuit has driven her to master the intricacies of the brain's fear responses and to develop effective strategies for rapid and lasting change.

Meg's expertise is rooted in cutting-edge, evidence-based methods for managing anxiety, overcoming fear of failure, and combating burnout. Her advanced training with renowned figures such as Jack Canfield, Ken Honda, Dr. Edna Foa, and Cloe Madanes, along with her certifications in Emotional Freedom Technique (EFT) and as an Advanced Canfield Success Trainer, equip her with specialized skills for fostering self-compassion and creating fulfilling lives.

Focused on transforming outdated notions of success and converting fear into genuine fulfillment, Meg underscores the importance of supportive environments and positive influences. She demonstrates that achieving significant change can be quick, gentle, and long-lasting.

Driven by a deep commitment to helping others rewire their minds for happiness, Meg advocates for compassionate self-care and the potential for everyone to live joyfully and purposefully. When she's not helping others transform their lives, Meg is traveling, attending retreats, and spending quality time with her family, friends, dogs, cat, and turtle.

For personalized guidance to unlock your full potential, creating a life filled with purpose and joy, contact Meg at megmcsherry.com.

CHAPTER 15

OWN YOUR AWESOME!

*Why the Secret to Life Is in Finding
and Choosing the Light*

By Miranda VonFricken

his is a story about the light. A personal, yet universal one of resilience, full of ups, downs, and the unimaginable realities that life often throws at us, but mostly about the light. Unfortunately light, no matter how encountered, cannot be revealed or experienced without the darkness. This duality of the human experience is one I have lived with more than most.

This story is full of darkness, death, and rejection, but also of love, renewal, and a personal decision that changed it all.

IN THE BEGINNING

I was like any young professional, excited to make her mark on the world, eager to show them all what I was made of—sparkles and unlimited possibility, and armed with more positive affirmations than any one woman should be. I spent years climbing the corporate ladder, praised and promoted for my dedication, innovative solutions, and way with people that would motivate unprecedented results. I was three years into a position some would call a dream job—I certainly did. I loved it so much I put my life coaching and speaking business on hold to go all in. I spent my days leading talent acquisition and leadership development efforts for a global organization and my evenings creating opportunities to elevate and expand my role and the people I served.

It seemed as if I had found my happy, both personally and professionally, sharing often with my network on LinkedIn. Mondays were my favorite. I'd create a post inspiring other professionals online and call it "Motivational Monday." It was a hit!

Until one particular Monday in February 2018.

My little brother Jack, just nineteen years old, lost his life in a tragic accident.

He was one of my favorite people in this entire world; funny, handsome, and full of unlimited potential. He would light up a room just by walking in. Jack was born when I was eighteen, so I often felt like one of his parents – because of that we had a bond stronger than a typical brother and sister.

Losing him felt like a piece of my soul had been cut out. My heart was broken; I couldn't imagine a world without him. As I grieved this unimaginable loss, I had no idea the professional life I spent years dedicated to was about to disappear as well.

One week after returning from bereavement, my position was eliminated.

I was told it was a "business decision," but all I felt was loss, again.

Over the next several weeks I struggled with my identity, my purpose, and my faith. It got dark—real dark. I'd wake up tired, spend my days in a fog, and nights weren't any better. I felt empty; confused as to why God would take my brother and kick me while I was down by taking my career too.

Over the next several years, I found myself confronting a truth that eventually touches all of us: life is an unrelenting balancing act of highs and lows. None of us escapes the inevitability of change.

Yet, despite it all, this is a story of light, hope, and an unwavering quest to be one with the light.

I consider it all a blessing—to be part of this duality of life's beauty, and its pain. Or as I lovingly call it: the "good, bad, ugly, and awesome."

But this is just the beginning, and as it turns out I was in for an awakening I could never have imagined.

MEANT FOR MORE

Losing Jack wasn't my first experience losing a loved one. I previously lost two sets of grandparents and had a near-fatal medical experience with my husband. It wasn't until losing someone so young that I realized how unpredictable life actually is. I questioned my faith, wondering why God would do this to our family.

I consulted friends and members of my church for answers. I shared with someone how upset I was with God, and the guilt I felt because of it. She reassured me it was OK saying, "He can take it"—hearing that gave me relief I hadn't felt in months.

While in mourning, I stopped doing a lot of the things I loved, specifically connecting with people and sharing posts on LinkedIn. When I felt ready to hop back on, to my surprise, I noticed hundreds of messages from connections and non-connections, expressing their concern and wondering why I disappeared. I was touched and decided to write a post sharing my loss and how I was feeling. That set off a chain of events that led to what would happen next.

In my heart, I knew I was meant for more. The feeling I had sharing my content and the interaction that followed set off a spark of recognition in my soul that said, "This is why you're here. To share your heart, to guide others through tough challenges, to lead." My former side hustle of coaching and speaking was calling me once again.

I leaned in. I listened. I took action. Only this time, I knew I had to do it with God as my divine business partner. I wasn't exactly sure what it would look like, but I knew it was time to get back out there. I invested in myself, taking courses, listening to uplifting podcasts, and spending time with friends and family. I prayed – a lot! I talked to Jack; I gave myself grace. I focused on healing my heart, my relationship with God, and my new way of living.

GOING ALL IN

In December 2019, after two more "position eliminations" I felt it was time to go all in on my entrepreneurial journey. I had the vision, drive, and support of my family.

Three months later the pandemic hit.

What should have sent me into a panic ended up propelling me forward.

Because no one could meet in person, I started hosting virtual meetups. My goal was to keep the business community connected. Shortly after, companies started asking me to speak at *their* virtual events and teach their teams how to use LinkedIn. I launched a course of my own and started helping individuals and organizations stay connected and engaged during this time—I started to feel like me again, and...I was officially a full-time entrepreneur.

My new coaching and consulting business replaced my corporate salary and I felt completely free!

By 2023 I'd built a multiple six-figure business, was named a Women of Empowerment by the YWCA of Northeastern NY and became a two-time International Women's Day Speaker. After a little encouragement I started a podcast called *Own Your Awesome*, where I shared my experience as an entrepreneur and woman of faith spreading words of wisdom on topics such as leadership, social media, sales, money, and more! I was living the life I had dreamed of creating and feeling closer to God every day.

It had seemed that I cracked the code of life after loss.

Then, on August 5, my phone rang.

My twenty-one-year-old brother, Vinny, was rushed to the hospital after collapsing.

It was a heart attack. He didn't survive.

I could feel my body shutting down. No way was God taking another brother.

I couldn't do this again!

We just celebrated his college graduation, he accepted his first job offer and was in love with his college sweetheart, how is this reality?

It turns out, that while my business was thriving during the pandemic, his heart was deteriorating due to long-form COVID, and we had no idea.

The shock was too much for me, the grief threatened to take every ounce of faith I had, but I thought of my husband and our children, and I refused to let them experience me drown in darkness again. This time, I vowed to handle my grief completely differently. Not because the loss was different, but because I was.

I took a beat. I prayed more than I ever had. Then, one night, there was a moment I felt my brothers with me. It was the most surreal feeling of love and comfort. I took solace in knowing they were together. It didn't take away my pain, but it did bring a little peace to my heart.

Choosing the Light

I learned through my years of healing that life is 10 percent what happens and 90 percent how you respond to it. So I figured, if life was going to double its efforts on knocking me down, I would double mine on climbing back up.

And that meant going all in on my faith more than ever.

I invested in courses and coaches that focused on spirituality, faith, and intuition. I worked with professionals in multiple modalities of healing such as energy and light work, and dove into learning Kabbalah – this brought so much clarity and more awareness of my soul and its journey than any other practice I've been a part of.

I also started to share my faith more openly in professional settings—starting a live LinkedIn show called *15 Minutes of Faith*, where I share my journey of healing, prayer, and my love for Jesus and His teachings.

Doubling down on my faith was a conscious decision I made after experiencing more loss than anyone should have. This decision has led to more joy than I could ever have imagined. It's changed who I surround myself with, how I do business, and why I'm on this Earth. My walk with God, both personally and professionally is the best decision I've ever made. Choosing Him, choosing the light wasn't easy, but it was inevitable.

Since making this decision, my life and business have soared to great heights. I've become a best-selling author, built a thriving consultancy and coaching practice, established a popular brand and podcast, and experienced the kind of magic I used to dream of.

I've found that the path to rising again is paved with purpose and I've channeled my pain, loss, and strength into helping others. As the founder of Own Your Awesome!—a global movement dedicated to empowering women to live out and shine a light on their calling—I rise, so they can too. I am a practice-what-I-preach kind of gal, and my clients know when I say they can do something, it's because I've done it myself.

Every day, I make the conscious choice to choose the light, and I'll spend my life guiding others to do the same. It's not easy, but it's a choice anyone can make.

No matter what life throws at us, I've learned that when you choose the light, you can face anything. There are a few steps I teach, but the first thing you need is to be open to the light and what connecting with it can do to your life. From there you can use these three steps to change your life and destiny!

1. Decide.

Any great transformation begins with a decision. It's the spark that ignites the journey. You must make the conscious decision to transform, to heal, to fight. Whatever the case may be—decide, and you're halfway there.

The act of deciding is profound. It's a declaration to yourself and the Universe that you're ready to embrace the journey ahead, no matter how challenging it might be. It's a decision only you can make. It's a private act within yourself.

When you choose the light, you're choosing faith over fear, hope over despair, and ultimate happiness over temporary satisfaction. This decision sets the intention and the foundation for everything that follows. It's a commitment to yourself just as much as the light.

Choosing the light is about recognizing that while we can't always control what happens to us, we can control how we respond. It's about understanding that setbacks, losses, and hardships are part of the journey, but they don't define us. What defines us is how we rise, how we find the strength to continue, and how we keep moving forward.

Once you make this decision, it's almost impossible to not make it happen. The power of intention is incredible. By deciding to choose the light, you align your thoughts, actions, and energy towards positive outcomes. This decision will guide your actions, shape your mindset, and attract the support and opportunities you need to succeed.

2. Activate it.

Once you've decided to choose the light, that's when the real work begins. Making the decision is a powerful first step, but it's the consistent actions that follow which truly transform your life. This is the time to immerse yourself in your decision and call in the resources and support that will help you move forward.

Choosing the light is an ongoing journey, requiring dedication, effort, and resilience. It's about seeking out ways to nurture and sustain your commitment to positivity and growth. For me, this journey involved hiring a coach, taking courses, reading books, and adjusting my environment and routines.

Hiring a coach provided guidance when I needed clarification, or the accountability needed to stay on track. Taking courses opened my mind to new possibilities. Reading books offered wisdom and deepened my commitment to the light. Adjusting my environment and habits helped take my decision to the next level.

Remember, the journey of choosing the light is a personal one—it's also one that's ongoing. It requires you to continuously seek out resources and engage in practices that support your growth. By doing so, you create a life that's not only filled with light but also inspires others to choose the light for themselves.

3. Share it!

Deciding to choose the light and going all in on activating it is an incredible journey—don't be shy about it! As your spiritual confidence grows, so will your desire to share this transformation with everyone you encounter. This journey isn't just about personal growth; it's about becoming a beacon for others, illuminating the path, and inspiring them to embark on their own journeys toward the light.

When you choose the light, the changes within you are noticeable. Your energy shifts, and your presence radiates positivity. Friends, family, and even strangers will notice a "lighter" you. They'll see the joy in your eyes, the peace in your demeanor, and the strength in your spirit. They'll become curious and ask what you've been doing. This is your opportunity to share your journey. Don't keep this a secret. Light is meant to shine!

OWN YOUR AWESOME!

Every day, I choose the light. Every day, I activate that decision by taking bold action toward my goals and leaning in to God's Word. Every day, I share my faith with those close to me and those new to me. These three things—decide, activate, and share—have led me to the most awesome life I could have ever imagined.

It turns out I have cracked the code to life after loss. It's in finding and choosing the light.

And I pray that my story inspires the same for you.

About Miranda

Miranda VonFricken loves Jesus, wears pink tutus, and missed her original calling to be an SNL/sitcom comedian, but says this life she's created is no consolation prize. It was divinely guided!

She is a former HR and higher-education executive, a LinkedIn strategist, and a personal branding evangelist, who's passionate about all things energy and abundance, and is credentialed and confident enough to charge her worth.

Miranda is the founder of Own Your Awesome!™, a podcast, bestselling book, and global movement attracting and expanding women at work, at home, and online!

With over fifteen years of leading teams to success in higher education, sales, and human resources, she stopped ignoring the call from her highest self and went all in on entrepreneurship. Since then, she has traveled the world connecting, coaching, and consulting students, entrepreneurs, executives, and organizations who are ready to *own their awesome* in their life, career, and business. With a passion for individual growth and performance elevation, Miranda has been coaching individuals and groups for over twenty years. She creates and conducts workshops on self-leadership, employee engagement, motivation, personal branding, social selling, and LinkedIn.

Miranda is a certified life and business coach, earned a master's in motivation from Empire State College, and has studied the Science of Happiness at Yale University. She's a two-time International Women's Day featured speaker and was named 2021 Woman of Empowerment.

Called to elevate every woman who has a story, a brand, or a dream and help them shine so bright it'll be impossible to ignore and achieve. If she's not on stage speaking at a women's conference or corporate event, you'll find her on Zoom changing the lives of her mastermind groups and community members.

She's a wife, a (sports) mom of two, and a positive force in her online and international community.

To learn more about Miranda and her services, visit https://MirandaVonFricken.com and be sure to connect with her on LinkedIn!

CHAPTER 16

THE BLESSING OF ADVERSITY

Embrace Change; Find Purpose; Achieve Success

By Patrick Mancuso

The phone rang, cutting through the typical noise that comes with the household of a busy family.

My wife was pregnant and reaching full term. Her doctor was calling to inform us that test results showed the presence of preeclampsia, a dangerous condition that posed a major threat to both my wife and our unborn baby. We were told to head to the emergency room immediately. It's fairly common, so at first, we saw no need to panic. We were wrong. I sat in the hospital for days as my son's condition worsened and during that time, I received another phone call. It was one of my business partners, his voice urgent and insistent. He needed to meet me immediately, right there in the hospital. Two phone calls. Two shocks. Both of which forever altered the course of my life. It's startling how a single moment—a phone call, a routine errand, a chance meeting—can irrevocably change everything. For me those calls brought harsh truths and painful lessons, but they also became the catalyst for a journey toward joy and fulfillment. At that moment, however, gratitude was a distant thought.

I was engulfed in anger, shock, and devastation.

I started my career in real estate in 1990 and had joined Keller Williams in 2002. I had hit the coveted goal of building a "mega agent" team and enjoying huge success which parlayed into a leadership role spearheading company expansion into new markets. We started small, with just eleven agents but as president and CEO of a Minnesota franchise, my team and I grew the firm to eight hundred agents in just four years.

It was a time of tremendous growth and recognition, but it all came to a screeching halt that day in 2006 when my world was cut into two distinct periods—before the phone calls, and after.

The day my wife was admitted to the hospital, I sat in the waiting room and picked up a newspaper. The top article headline read, "60% of Couples Who Lose a Child Divorce." I had no idea the impact of that article at the time; however, I quickly discovered why and the plan God had for me and my family.

The second most devasting call of my life came five days later. It was one of the regional leaders at Keller Williams. He said we needed to meet and made it clear that it could not wait. He came to the emergency room to tell me that behind the scenes of the agency, relationships had gone sour. When he finally cut to the chase, I learned that the business I had built was cutting me out.

Not only that, but as the news of the structural unraveling circulated through the industry, I would be the scapegoat. He wasn't just there to deliver the bad news, but to offer some guidance on how to preserve my reputation. He suggested I take full responsibility, which seemed preposterous to me, and I never did get to tell my side of the story. Yet, the anger and grief I felt from being blindsided by my partners was nothing compared to what happened next.

Ten days after my son was born, we would have to make the gut-wrenching decision to remove him from life support.

THE GIFT OF STARTING OVER

There's something that happens to us when our life is cut in half. We become intentional about everything. It finally hits us how vulnerable we are and how short life is, so we finally wise up and rethink our foundational values.

We decide what's important and what's not; what we will tolerate and what we won't. If we really learned from our trauma, we'll weigh every future decision against this value system and act accordingly.

Over time I was able to let go of how I felt I was wronged. My wife and I remained strong together and in 2007 on Christmas day we had a healthy baby girl. I learned the importance of balance. I learned the value of aligned partnerships and remembered the guidance of one of my mentors, Dar Reedy, co-founder of one of the most successful independent real estate companies in North America at that time and the firm at which I started my real estate journey. He shared with me the philosophy of the book *What People Think of You Is None of Your Business*.

Once I freed myself from defining my success by the perception of others, I was able to fully move forward into a new and fulfilling purpose.

It took me many months to negotiate my buy out. In 2009 I was approached to be a part of a program born from the financial collapse of real estate. It was a bootcamp teaching agents the core elements of success. We traveled to different cities over a seven-week period and it was a huge success. Over the next several years, I was a coach in that program, then the head of coaches, then director of sales and ultimately, we took 170,000 agents through this bootcamp. While the curriculum was designed to improve results in real estate, it was based on mindset principles applicable to every area of life.

The best part was that in order to teach the core tools of the program, I had to live them. In doing so, I learned that God always has a plan. I had gone through one of the darkest, most difficult things a human being can go through and that meant I understood heartache, healing and transformation in a way that made me a very strong coach.

So in 2020, when COVID hit and it was time to shift again, I decided to focus full time on growing the consulting company I had started years earlier. Once I made that decision, I grew to eight million dollars over an eighteen-month period. My team and I help business owners prepare, protect and prosper in their business. Over my years as a coach in the bootcamp, I worked with twelve thousand business owners and entrepreneurs and I learned that there are a few challenges most of us have in common:

We lack a solid vision, we move forward without a roadmap, and our minds can be our worst enemies!

I started my company with the goal of helping people solve those problems so they could build businesses and lives that set them free. I developed the Mancuso Method of business leadership and while it is designed to help our clients change their companies, it inevitably changes their lives, and I believe it could change yours too.

It's just three simple steps: prepare, protect, and prosper.

1. Prepare.

Research consistently shows 90 percent or more of people who set goals do not achieve them. Although this is a shocking number, it is easy to understand why. It has to do with our brains and how we are built as human beings.

Over the years, I've had over thirty-five thousand coaching and consulting conversations with people from all walks of life and businesses. I would say, "Tell me about your goals." Almost within seconds they would say, "I want to sell X, or I want to earn X." The action of setting a goal comes so naturally for most. Goal setting is the easy part.

In most cases to achieve a goal, one must take a different action and change a current behavior. This is where the process begins to break down. Human beings do not naturally embrace change. In fact, we fight it. Even though logically we realize it means we likely will not achieve the goal. Let me give you an example.

You're driving down a road that you've driven down thousands of times, and you see a Road Closed sign. As you look beyond the road-closed sign, you don't see any construction equipment or workers. It appears no pavement has been disturbed. So, one's initial thought is, "No, that road isn't closed." You then decide to drive beyond the road-closed sign only to discover the road is truly closed beyond the signs. This is an example of fighting change even though it's obvious that we must change course to move forward. Once we set a new goal, we must now do something *different*, which will be uncomfortable. In fact, just the thought of having to take action will push our brain into a protective mode. Now it becomes a whole different conversation about the goal we just set. Think about it, within minutes we went from excitement about the new goal we set, to fear about what it will now take to achieve it.

So how do we get around this and get where we want to go?

As a consultant, my job is to get our clients focused on the most important step in the process, first; focusing on the benefits and impact of achieving the goal is critical. What do we get to do, experience, or give because we succeeded? There is also an impact on others around us, whether that is our immediate family, friends, community, coworkers, etc. Goal achievement has impacts far and wide. Then by correlation, when we do not achieve goals, the impacts are far and wide. So, let's put a ribbon on this. When you set a goal, don't focus on what it's going to take to make it happen. Focus on what achieving that goal does for you and others around you. Why would that be important to you? How would you feel? Why is that feeling important to you? How would achieving the goal make others feel?

Once you're clear on that, do your homework! When I left my original broker in 2002, I entered into a business partnership with seven other people, but I hadn't done my due diligence. Had I done my research into their work history I probably would have noticed some misalignments and chosen differently.

The best way to find clarity and the confidence to go full speed ahead with your decisions is to clearly identify your goals, timeline, strategy, and stakeholders.

Once you've got that dialed in, it's time to protect your legacy.

2. Protect what you've built.

This is the part that most people skip right over. They set a goal, they reach that goal and at that point, they think their work is done. When I was pushed out of the agency I helped to build, I realized very quickly that my family and I were totally vulnerable. Of course, if I had to do it over again, I would have made sure to set things up in such a way that my bank account, and legacy, were protected.

Most people are not schooled in what it takes to protect their assets. It's just not their lane. They don't understand the importance of fine print. They might not understand the nuances of tax mitigation or how to pay their fair share and no more. Imagine there's a tax credit that allows business owners to reduce the taxes they pay by $15,000 a year. If they own that business for twenty years, that's $300,000 in savings! Those are the kind of things consultants like me are trained to know.

And what if something happens to you? Do you have enough insurance? Is it clearly spelled out who gets what or are you leaving your family in a lurch?

My own experience taught me the importance of having safeguards in place. It's not just about building something great; it's about protecting it, ensuring its longevity, and securing a future for those you love. Only then can you feel safe in moving to the next step: prosper!

3. Prosper.

When I first joined Keller Williams, they had a very limited marketing plan to market franchises. That was crazy to me. Our two largest competitors controlled 80 percent of the market share. I knew we had to do things right at a high level, so I hired a marketing firm to put a plan together. It worked because it was a *system*. Systems scale businesses. When I began to focus fulltime on my consulting business, we worked with more than eight hundred business owners over an eighteen-month period and my entire team consisted of myself and a director of operations. We did so well because strategically I understand how to connect dots. Every business has leverage points. Three of the most important are systems, people and tools. When you leverage those things, you can grow faster than you ever thought possible.

Money is another tool. I can leverage it to buy business, and leverage businesses to create income. I can leverage time to accomplish more work in fewer hours. It's simple, yet most people don't take time to think logically about it. I don't cut my own lawn. The guys I pay to do it get the job done in about seven minutes when it would likely take me an hour or more. My dollar-per-hour rate that I earn in my business is way more than I pay for lawn mowing, so I would rather have that hour of my time back to spend on other things.

What are you doing that is stealing time and money from you? And how can you leverage, delegate or systematize it to make the best use of your resources?

Figure that out, and you'll be well on your way to rapid and predictable growth. Then all you've got to do is hold on to it.

What It Really Means to Succeed

Most people in the world define success by dollars and titles. But if you look up the actual dictionary definition of the word however, it is "a desired outcome." Most of the time, it's not that we want to make a million dollars for the sake of having a million dollars but for the freedom it provides.

We want it so we can build a better life for our families, check some things off the bucket list or maybe gain control of our time. Ultimately, success is attained when you achieve the desired outcome *underneath* the goal.

It's never just about the money. At my company, we often say that what you don't know can cost you commas and zeros, but the truth is, what you don't know can also cost you time, joy and peace of mind.

Ask yourself what goal you would be excited to prepare for, what you would fight to protect and what you'd be proud to prosper in. And then gather resources, plans, and experts to help you achieve it.

The reality is, you have no idea when a phone call, a trip to the grocery store, or an unscheduled meeting will turn your life upside down. We can't control the curveballs life throws at us, but we can control how we live each day, preparing for the unexpected, cherishing every moment, and living by our own carefully crafted and thoughtfully designed definition of massive success!

About Patrick

Pat Mancuso is a distinguished entrepreneur, business coach, and consultant recognized for his strategic expertise and dedication to empowering business owners. With a career of over three decades, Pat has amassed over forty thousand hours of coaching and consulting experience, demonstrating a profound understanding of the entrepreneurial landscape. He has been named Coach of the Year twice within one of the largest real estate companies in the world, underscoring his exceptional skills and impact.

At the helm of Mancuso Consulting Group, Pat developed the transformative 360 Mancuso Method, designed to help business owners Prepare, Protect, and Prosper. This method addresses the core challenges faced by entrepreneurs, providing them with tailored strategies to enhance business growth, safeguard assets, and achieve personal financial freedom.

Pat's extensive experience enables him to mentor business owners effectively, guiding them through complex business environments with a focus on operational efficiency, strategic planning, and succession planning. His approach is holistic, aligning business objectives with personal goals to ensure sustainable success.

A sought-after speaker and thought leader, Pat frequently shares his insights on various platforms, including his podcast, *Destination Business Freedom*, where he discusses pivotal business strategies with industry experts. His engaging style and actionable advice make him a favorite among audiences seeking practical solutions to real-world business problems.

Pat is also a leadership behavioral specialist, using his expertise to help leaders understand and optimize their behavioral traits for better team dynamics and overall performance. His professional network is vast, spanning multiple industries and geographies, which he utilizes to provide clients with diverse perspectives and innovative solutions.

In addition to his professional achievements, Pat is deeply committed to his community, actively participating in philanthropic efforts and mentoring aspiring entrepreneurs. His passion for helping others succeed is the driving force behind his work, making him a trusted advisor and partner in the journey to business excellence.

171

Beyond his professional life, Pat finds joy in personal pursuits. He enjoys playing golf and has a keen interest in high-performance cars. He also enjoys spending time with his family and engaging in outdoor activities that recharge his spirit. This balance of professional dedication and personal fulfillment is a testament to his belief in a holistic approach to success.

For more information about Pat Mancuso and his services, visit www.mancusocg.com or connect with him on LinkedIn at www.linkedin.com/in/patmancuso.

CHAPTER 17

THE POWER OF JOY

El Tango te Espéra—Anibal Troilo
("The tango awaits you.")

───────────

By Eulalia Codipietro

was hopping through the dining room when the music coming from the TV caught my attention. Its rhythm seemed to pass through my skin, straight to my heart, and as I turned to look, a flash of red moved across the screen. A vibrant, bewitching dancer swirled in the arms of her partner in a dynamic tango, and I was overwhelmed with emotion, a passionate feeling coursing through my veins, so much that in that moment, I forgot about my father's health issues. I was swept away by the dancers, and for the length of that tango I was joyful, wild, and free.

Suddenly an invisible hand seemed to grab me by the collar of my wool knit sweater and pull me back into reality.

"Silly girl," said the voice of my inner critic. "You can't do it. You're not good enough. The tango is dangerous. Let it go."

That's how, at the age of nine, I sabotaged myself and buried my biggest dream in a bunker deep inside.

The desire to dance nagged me for years, but my parents made it clear that the arts were not a viable profession.

Instead, I would be made to study math, a subject that was a stark contrast to my passions.

I studied hard, but the words and equations were a jumbled mix in my head; a foreign language that I could not grasp. I struggled terribly and received low scores on my assessments which only validated the voice of my inner critic who reminded me I

173

would never be good enough to succeed. I tried to repeat words of encouragement to myself but continued to fail.

One day as I studied Aristotle, a light bulb came on!

Aristotle wrote that the difference between two distinct objects (e.g., a chair and a table) made from the same raw material (e.g., the same block of wood), was not the material itself, but the way in which the material had been shaped.

This led to two conclusions: firstly, the potential function given to one object or another was not only a consequence of the material, but also of the form.

Secondly, the change of function from table to chair was the result of inertia.

I realized that my brain was made of the same material as the brains of the most mathematically gifted classmates. If there was no difference between my brain matter and theirs, what was the form that conditioned my ability to deal with mathematics? The answer was my thinking. If I wanted to change my mathematical destiny, I would have to change the way I think about myself in relation to it.

So I made these resolutions:

1. Every day, I would claim that I'm just as smart as the mathematically gifted students in my class.

2. I'd look at the reasons for my difficulties and find the appropriate answers.

3. I'd train relentlessly to meet every challenge.

I diligently adhered to this formula, and I began to pass my math exams with high marks!

I now knew that when tough situations arose in my life, I could change how I thought about them, overcome the difficulty, and get the results I wanted.

Little did I know how valuable that skill would become.

A DANCE WITH DESTINY

I kept my dream of dancing the Argentinian tango buried deep within me, casting it aside as nothing more than a childhood fantasy. But a chance encounter in Paris was about to remind me that some dreams never die.

Walking up the Trocadero, my partner, my daughter and I came across a group of people dancing nearby. The rhythm of the music drew me in, and the movement of the dancers' bodies stirred me from a deep spiritual sleep. I stood there, mesmerized, but my companion was bored and hurried me along. My feet walked with him, but a piece of my heart remained forever with the dancers.

Nine months later, to my surprise, he asked me out. A dance event was taking place at a venue in our capital city. "And what dance is on offer that evening?", I asked.

"The tango!" he exclaimed enthusiastically.

I froze. It was one thing to let the poetry take you away in a foreign city, but here at home it felt deeply painful. I gave into going on the condition that we watch for a short time.

The melody that night was sad, reflecting the pain I felt watching from the sidelines.

"Here she is!" my companion suddenly exclaimed, "She's the colleague who advised me to come here."

A strange feeling came over me. Why was he suddenly interested in tango gatherings?

Two months later he asked for a separation. He had found true love...with the colleague who invited us to tango.

A deep rage swept over me, not only because he had betrayed me, but because at 9 years old, I had started the cycle of betraying myself. I made a promise to myself in that moment: I would take back my joy and become a professional tango dancer.

THE MUSIC STOPS, BUT NOT FOR LONG

The chair is wooden, and I shift uncomfortably.

Three years after that night, I am sitting in a wing of the hospital dedicated to treatment of degenerative immune diseases. The humidity is oppressive, and this entire day is beginning to feel like a slow descent into hell.

But I can't leave.

Because I'm losing my sight, and I don't know why.

Finally, the doctor calls my name. For some reason, I'm comforted by his smart-looking glasses, but my comfort is short-lived as I see him frowning at the documents on his desk.

"Madam," he said, in a very indifferent tone that only practiced deliverers of bad news can master, "you have Multiple Sclerosis."

I was stunned but knew immediately that he was wrong.

Yes, I had a damaged optic nerve. Yes, I was tired and needed rest, but no, this disease was not in my body.

"I disagree." I said stubbornly.

"Madam," he said in a tone reserved for those who are in denial of reality, "50 percent of optic neuritis cases are caused by MS."

"Great," I said, completely unmoved. "I am the other 50 percent."

He shook his head in frustration. "The remaining half comes from a myriad of other factors, each accounting for a tiny percentage: it is on the order of the rare."

"Ah," I thought. He just said the magic word, the word that described the sequence of events in my life so far, the word I would eventually use to describe my own response to life's ebbs and flows.

Rare.

An Early Dance with Adversity

It was not surprising that I landed in that doctor's office.

I was born on high alert.

A few days into my mother's pregnancy, my parents were in a car accident. I survived, but the shock seemed to fuse into me. A few weeks later my mother nearly miscarried, but I survived. By the age of a year and a half I was displaying signs of depression and at eight, my father had suffered his first coma.

He was sick for years and it planted a deep-rooted terror within me that he could be taken at any moment.

My early life was defined by this fear, by family conflict and by the death of a dear cousin of multiple sclerosis at just nineteen years of age.

Adulthood brought little comfort. I had a daughter I adored but had a very challenging relationship with her father. I fell into exhaustion from the emotional turmoil, ended up becoming a single mother, had to sell my home, contracted Covid, moved in the aftermath of selling our family house, and lost count of how many times I had to dig for the seed of resilience within me so I could be there for my child when all I really wanted to do was fall apart.

Was it any wonder I had landed in a hospital, my body finally rebelling against this constant turmoil?

"Your body is losing control," said the doctor, "You'll have to get used to the idea."

I froze in terror. I had accepted that I had no control over others, but I could not accept that I had no control over myself. This sickness was threatening to sideline my dream and kill my source of joy.

I scanned my body and felt I wasn't sick. I was mentally and emotionally exhausted. But I was going to live.

As I left his office, I concentrated my efforts on just one question: What should I do now?

The answer appeared immediately. I would heed the words one of the greatest tango maestros in the world had said: "Professional dancers dance in all circumstances."

So that was my decision. I was going to dance that night and, no matter what the future brought, I would keep dancing. I had spent long enough in darkness.

It was time to live for joy.

That night, still reeling from the diagnosis that threatened to end my dream, I danced with total abandon and allowed my body to move however it wanted to.

I was *alive*!

As the end of my relationship loomed over me and I wrestled with the fact that I'd have to create a new life, it hit me: If all those years ago I could retrain my brain for math, which was not in any way a passion of mine, imagine how far I could go with the things I was passionate about!

I recognized that the barriers I'd built as a child were constructed from fear, a weapon to protect me from the pain of failure. With this mental barrier removed, I could move forward pursuing my dreams.

From the moment I began to dance the tango, my level of joy increased, and doors opened in every aspect of my life.

I would need that joy for what was about to happen next.

ANOTHER DANCE, ANOTHER DISCOVERY

The consultant specializing in neuroplastic rebalancing was asking me to recount the episodes of my life that brought me to see him.

I was dancing regularly now, but despite my good mood and positive attitude, my brain was still collapsing under stress of the separation and fear around the MS diagnosis had begun to creep in.

The consultant confirmed that my symptoms were consistent with PTSD and my brain displayed Asperger's traits. It was like lightning had struck!

I won't say I was happy to hear it, but the shock was followed by an odd sense of relief. I recognized that knowing my neurodiverse nature set me free. It empowered me to clearly describe my behavior, accept it and take responsibility for it.

It totally explained my unintended contribution to my two separations and my tendency to isolate myself.

I was suddenly aware of myself in a whole new way! Looking back at the thread of my life, every time I had to start over, or overcome a challenge or process a pivot I never saw coming, I had pulled myself through with four things: awareness, alignment, action, and *joy*!

Cultivating Awareness and Alignment

In tango, staying aware is crucial to maintaining a connection with your partner. It's also a skill that has helped me avoid doom and gloom perspectives.

When I received the MS diagnosis, I was determined to stay aware of the truth. The truth was, I could be totally healthy and still die of an accident in the street. Health and immortality were illusory concepts. This awareness helped me make the fear of death redundant and kept me rooted in the present moment, where I could fully live and follow my dreams.

With discovering my Asperger's traits, I developed an awareness of my own behaviors and how they might be perceived, which shifted my inner dialogue. I was softer on myself and more patient. The better I understood my own view of the world, the happier I was living in it.

I became aware that for me, joy comes through alignment. When my spiritual, intellectual, emotional and physical worlds are coherent, wonderful things unfolded and I felt deep joy. Joy, it turned out, was my secret to the law of attraction.

What are you doing when you feel aligned, balanced and joyful? Whatever it is, the more you do it, the more you expand your field of attraction, and the more miracles you manifest!

Taking Courageous Action

There are no results without action.

Positive results are generated by acting with joy.

As I reflected on my life, I realized that the absence of awareness, alignment, and joy led to decisions, choices, and actions that took me away from a life of fulfillment, and success.

I realized that it was not life that had been preventing me from getting what I wanted. It was me. I had mastered my fear of math, become a dancer, and begun to heal my health. I had before me the proof that I did not lack the power to manifest what I wished, as I had believed for so long, but that I had forgotten my great power to manifest anything. All I needed was to give it my full attention. The direction my life took was entirely my choice—a life of dreams or a life of despair.

So I would choose joy—and I would choose myself!

The Universe Winks at Us

Healing is not a linear journey. One evening while preparing to go out to dance, I questioned if I'd done enough to heal my past betrayal and truly move forward.

That's when the universe winked at me!

I dressed in a black tango dress for a festive evening of dancing. A lottery was planned in celebration of the upcoming Christmas holidays and I deeply desired to win.

The organizers asked me to help with the raffle. I was to draw the two winning tickets, one for a bottle of Argentinian red wine, the other for a bottle of Crémant luxe bourgeois.

Holding the velvet pouch with one hand, I stirred the folded pieces of paper and extracted the first ticket: number 25.

A tanguera seated in the back jumped for joy, waving her winning ticket. I pulled a second ticket. Number 36. Nobody presented themselves. I shook the bag again to shuffle the tickets and, feeling the joy of the evening, caught one of them, unfolded it, and read it aloud. Number 15.

I was stunned! I called my own number. *I had chosen myself!*

This was the lesson life had been trying to teach me for years: to win in life, you must dare to choose yourself.

My mission, then, would be to choose myself, every time.

And I hope you do too.

For there is nothing you can't overcome if you know your own power, if you lean in to joy, and if you always, without fail, choose yourself to win.

About Eulalia

For over two decades, Eulalia Codipietro has demonstrated a remarkable ability to reinvent herself and acquire a diverse range of skills. From mastering marketing strategy and communication to sales, product innovation, risk management, project execution, and leadership, Eulalia has built a solid foundation for her coaching and training business today. Her focus is on empowering women and organizations to harness the power of joy, enabling them to amplify their impact and achieve outstanding results.

As the founder and coach at MoveToJoy, Eulalia firmly believes that joy is the secret ingredient to success. She is on a mission to guide individuals in overcoming challenges, discovering their inner joy and creativity, and cultivating resilience in a way that is both effective and captivating. Eulalia's work as an international coach, mentor, consultant, and writer revolves around helping women tap into their inner resources, leading to a more fulfilling life through creative expression. She also works with organizations, fostering collaboration, diversity, and long-lasting relationships with their corporate talents.

Eulalia's coaching approach is a unique blend of mindset hacks, joy, and creativity tools that she has developed through her personal experiences and passions. While her expertise lies in career fulfilment, business development, and team collaboration, Eulalia has also delved into various topics, particularly those related to mindset and overcoming obstacles to achieve personal fulfillment. Her unwavering passion lies in witnessing people succeed and become the best versions of themselves.

While Eulalia finds joy in dancing the passionate Argentinian Tango and is actively pursuing this passion to transform it into an additional professional venture, she enjoys expressing herself through watercolor painting, and indulging in her love for writing fiction. As a proud mother to Emma, a teenager brimming with wisdom and humor, Eulalia shares a vibrant and fulfilling life with her daughter and their lively white Maltese, Joy.

Learn more:

- www.movetojoy.coach
- *Becoming a Champion of Joy* on Amazon

CHAPTER 18

NEVER GIVE UP

Resilience and Success in Life and Business

By Radim Pařík

The air was thick with sweat and anticipation as I locked eyes with my opponent, a worthy adversary with a calm and poised demeanor. We circled each other closely, each aware that every move must be intentional and precise. There was an unspoken respect, and even though I could feel sweat about to drip down from my forehead, I didn't dare take my eyes off him to brush it away.

We moved around each other, preparing to strike, our minds drawing on years of training and our bodies fueled by an inner fire that refused to be extinguished.

As the match went on, I felt a profound connection to my own body, to my opponent and to the art of karate itself. It is a testament to focus, wisdom and an unwavering pursuit of excellence.

I was a young kid at the time. I had no idea I would one day become an expert negotiator but when I did, the principles I learned from karate were vitally important. I stay calm under pressure, adapt quickly, navigate changing negative dynamics and can read the strategies and intentions of the person across the table.

Success, like karate, is a journey of continuous improvement, a path where the greatest battles are fought within.

In the art of negotiation, as in karate, victory is not just about winning—it's about mastering oneself, triumphing over seemingly impossible circumstances, and learning that you don't lose if you fail; you only lose if you quit.

A Rough Beginning to a Strong Ending

My father was a violent man but a prominent one.

When my mother finally left with me and my brother Roman, we were stripped of the privilege we enjoyed as a soldier's family. We lived in a run-down flat with no bathroom, no water, and no heating system, but what we did have was love and the fierce determination of our mother who refused to give up.

It was my mother's leadership that allowed me to rise from a poverty-stricken youth to become an author, speaker, philanthropist, business owner and lead negotiator for top politicians in my country.

She instilled in me an unwavering belief that where I began had no bearing on where I could go.

The same is true in high stakes negotiation.

Usually when a client comes to me, in their mind it is already too late. They believe that their business is already destroyed, their finances are already ruined, and their relationships are irreparably damaged. They are blind to any possible solution. My job is to reveal possibilities, and my success history is 100 percent in the past six years. I solve cases there are no solutions for.

I can do that because I have learned the secrets to unlocking success. The principles that led me to victory on the karate floor are the same ones that lead me to victory in the board room, and the same ones that can lead you to achieve any goal you put your mind to.

You've got to remember that the beginning is no indication of the end and use that knowledge to drive a relentless hunt for solutions.

I promise you there is a solution. Sometimes it is hiding under biases and resentment. Sometimes it is on the other side of a willingness to be vulnerable. Wherever it is, you can find it by remembering the following principles, and taking them with you wherever you go.

Shape your mindset: Never stop learning.

One of the most important elements of a karate match is being careful to remember that no matter how prepared you are, your opponent can always win. Never underestimate the person opposite you. They have likely trained and prepared just as much and possibly more than you.

If I'm smart, I will watch the opponent carefully, not to beat him but to *learn* from him. I am always endlessly curious about how he or she is operating, what he might do next and what drives him. And if what I'm doing isn't working, I learn from that and try a new strategy.

When I'm in a negotiation, I know that if someone isn't listening to me, it's my problem, not theirs. I know immediately that the tactics I'm deploying are falling flat and I need to adjust my strategy, change my tone and lean further into understanding what they really want and why.

It can never be about me. That might sound counterintuitive, as we all have goals we are trying to reach. Yet what you'll find is that the best way to reach your own goals is to help someone else reach theirs.

It's not easy. You may not like them. You may not share their values and your biases may stop you from being inclined to help them. But when the outcome of the negotiation saves lives, jobs, relationships and businesses, your opinion doesn't matter. What matters is that you find a solution and you do that by staying committed to learning. Find out what matters to them and paint a picture that makes it possible.

Ultimately, understanding the other person's motivations and fears equips you with the insight you need to create a safe path based on trust, emotional connection and find mutually beneficial solutions. This knowledge transforms the negotiation from a battle of wills and arguments into a collaborative problem-solving endeavor.

The more you can learn, the better you can lead.

Precision matters.

Sometimes in karate you get one chance to deliver a winning kick. Precision is imperative. Miss your mark, and your opponent has time to strike back!

Precision of a different kind is required in business interaction.

In a meeting or a negotiation, you've got to be precise with your attention. Think of the other party as a puzzle that must be solved. Notice every nuance, listen to every word, look for non-verbal hints that might tell you what they're thinking.

If you are distracted for a second, you might miss a vital clue to the one thing that could turn the negotiation in your favor.

One time I was in an intense meeting with a man who came in cold as ice. He walked in the room and the temperature seemed to drop ten degrees! I immediately started observing him and could tell that he was not interested in relationships, he was interested in business and money. People were not high on his priority list. Appealing to his empathy was not going to work because there didn't seem to be any! So, I adjusted my strategy. I shifted my tone from warm to cold and spoke his language and eventually he agreed to everything I was asking for. I listened carefully to his motivations until I understood, and then I said, "No one has ever helped you the way you needed. You've been on your own for everything." Afterward, he told me that no one had ever spoken so nicely to him in business. Yet I wasn't nice! I simply mirrored him which made him feel heard and understood. Sometimes, instead of trying to change the person you are speaking with, monitor them on their own playing field and understand their pains and fears. It creates an emotional resonance that gives you the upper hand.

In the distracted world we live in, people are not used to precise attention. Not only is your interest in them a sign of respect, but it is also an effective strategy. Like a precise jab they don't know is happening and won't see coming, your focused attention will catch them by surprise, and may shift the tides in your favor.

Overconfidence bias

In karate, overconfidence is the kiss of death.

The minute you feel you feel you are invincible, you are vulnerable, and your opponent will notice and exploit every opening they see. When you are overconfident, you lose focus, you lose efficiency, and you lose matches. Years ago, I learned the hard way that humility keeps you balanced, while overconfidence sends you crashing to the mat...and into the pavement.

I was just 19 years old and felt like I could do anything in the world. I had no fear, and my training had instilled confidence in me that at some point crossed a line into arrogance. I felt untouchable and it was that feeling that compelled me to drive too fast down a highway, lose control and end up in a horrific crash that nearly left me paralyzed.

I'll never forget the terrifying feeling of waking up in the hospital unable to move. I couldn't even shower alone and the doctor said I would never run again. I refused to accept that. My mother sat by my side every day for six months and poured her belief into me. I never once thought to myself, "This isn't fair" because the reality is, it *was* fair. It was the direct result of arrogance. I recovered, but I didn't make that mistake again.

Overconfidence bias is a dangerous trap.

You fail to see danger when it's right in front of you. When you are so sure of yourself, you cannot anticipate what might happen next and because of that, you lose your edge.

Today, after every conversation, whether it's with a family member or an executive at the negotiation table, I go through my own debriefing procedure and ask myself these questions:

1. What worked tactically well?

2. What was the game changer?

3. What *didn't* work tactically well? It's not about self-punishment, it's about finding the potential for improvement.

4. What did I forget?

5. What did the other side do better?

6. What must I change next time?

There is a fine line between confidence, arrogance and gambling with business, people or your own life, and the wisest among us stay on the right side of it.

Manage your emotional bank account.

There is a common misconception in the business world that if you want to win and lead, you've got to be tough. The reality is that the strongest leaders understand the value of vulnerability.

Emotions are investments.

Just like with money, the more you invest, the higher the return.

I never look at the other party as an adversary, but rather as a human being. Everyone at the table has dreams, desires, fears and insecurities. Human behavior hasn't changed all that much in the last thousand years! We are motivated by safety, love, financial security, health and how people perceive us, how we appear in front of them. In the end, what drives each of us is the same thing that unites us... our humanity.

I respect everyone in the room, and I enter the conversation believing the best about them. The one thing all humans have in common is that we *feel*. People equate business with logic, but we don't make decisions based on logic. We make them based on emotion. You don't buy a car based on how many pounds of metal it is. You buy the car that excites you! You don't choose a mate based on how tall they are, you choose the one who inspires you.

If I want to appeal to the other party's emotions, I must be willing to be emotionally available too. It creates a sense of reciprocity and suddenly, they are sharing things with me they may not have had I remained stone-faced and tough.

True strength isn't found in keeping a tough exterior. In fact, it requires a great deal more courage to show our emotions than to tuck them away.

I've successfully led high stakes negotiations for everything from massively tense political situations to multimillion-dollar contract disputes. I do it by remembering that I am not working with data, evidence or numbers, but with *humans*.

Never give up.

If you look back at the lives of the most famous athletes in the world, or the most notable business leaders, you'll likely see that all of them had messy beginnings.

No one closes their first deal or wins their first match. Even Michael Jordan was cut from his high school basketball team!

I also know what it is like to have a humble and difficult beginning. But my mother taught me to never give up. In fact, I can't think of any book written that could teach me more than my mother did. As a kid, wading through the wreckage of poverty and divorce, she lifted me up and showed me what was possible. Her faith in me fueled my success.

So many people quit before the finish line because they fear repeating the failure they experienced in the beginning. They are focused on hitting a certain set of milestones rather than living by a certain set of values. I'm about to say something that might be controversial, but it's true. Conventional wisdom praises the setting of big goals, but the real key to success is knowing that it isn't about the goal itself at all. None of us knows if we will hit our goals. I wanted to be a doctor, and instead I became a negotiator. Did I fail because I never hit my original goal? Or did I succeed in living a life of impact and finding a purpose that was meant for me?

Success at its core is not about hitting a few milestones or making a million dollars. It's about the values you uphold and demonstrate along the way. At my company, our values are part of our non-negotiable policies.

We do not lie.

We are here to help.

It's never just about the money.

We don't measure our results by quarter or by year because our commitment to excellence knows no bounds and our character cannot be measured in data and spreadsheets, but in the continuation of our work.

Our focus is not on revenue, but on character and purpose. The revenue is a natural side-effect of living in integrity.

To this day I practice marital arts and the parallels between karate and life are never lost on me. Just as in karate, where discipline, perseverance, and respect are paramount, the journey to success is more about the values you uphold than the medals you win.

It's about leaving the mat as a better version of yourself than you were when you began.

Lastly, it's about remembering the importance of respect, for yourself, for others, and for the mission you were born to complete.

With love to my dearest ones.

To my mom: Thank you for making me a better person with your leadership than I could have ever been.

Thank you to my brother Roman for your unwavering support in every situation.

And thank you, my love of my life, for never leaving me even in the toughest moments.

About Radim

Radim Pařík is an international professional negotiator, lecturer, leader, and sign language inter-
preter. He serves as the president of the Association
of Negotiators and is a prolific speaker and author
featured prominently in Czech's media landscape.
Widely cited across television, radio, and newspapers, Radim stands as the most-cited negotiator in
the Czech Republic and Slovakia.

Radim is the acclaimed author of several books. Umění vyjednat
cokoliv *(The Art of Negotiating Anything)*, soared to best-seller status
within just five weeks of its release, and today it is the best-selling Czech
book on negotiation. Thanks to cowriting books *Empathetic Leadership*
and *Influence and Impact* with the master negotiator, Chris Voss, he also
became the world's best-selling author.

Born in the Czech Republic, Radim's journey has led him across bor-
ders. He resided in Germany and subsequently in Poland. In both these
countries he assumed prominent leadership roles within the multina-
tional Schwarz Group, an enterprise that *Forbes* recognizes as one of the
globe's top five largest retailers.

After obtaining his MSc and MBA in strategic management from
Nottingham Trent University, Radim earned his PhD in negotiation from
LIGS University, where he realized extensive research on the most effective tactics used during negotiations. He further honed his negotiation
skills through training under the guidance of multiple former FBI agents
and completed the Harvard Mediation Intensive and Harvard negotiation
program, culminating in his graduation from the Harvard Negotiation
Master Class. He is also a graduate of the Schranner Negotiation Institute
and Advanced High Performance Leadership at IMD University led by
George Kohlrieser.

Radim's educational achievements also include graduating from the
Certified Global Negotiator program at the University of St. Gallen,
Negotiation Program led by William Ury, as well as mastering negotiation techniques based on Mossad principles. He completed training in
negotiating with kidnappers and terrorists from the international negotiation organization The Trusted Agency, the Hermione program.

Radim led the negotiation program at several European universities.

He founded Radim Pařík's Fascinating Academy for commercial negotiation training. He is the co-owner of PR PA RT NE RS Advisory Group and initiated the Association of Negotiators, uniting professionals across five countries on four continents.

He actively supports the blind and deaf people, is an ambassador for children from orphanages, helps them transition into society, and teaches them how to negotiate. Radim aids TOP 100 Czech and Slovak companies for tough negotiations and lectures on negotiations for Security Information Service agents and top politicians. He earned the Czechoslovak LinkedIn Personality award.

Contact Radim:
Web: www.fascinating.academy
Email: fascinujte@fascinating.academy

Social Media:
Facebook: www.facebook.com/radim.parik
LinkedIn: www.linkedin.com/in/radim-parik
Instagram: www.instagram.com/radimparik

CHAPTER 19

UNLEASHING INNOVATION

The Power to Transform, Ignite, Disrupt!™

By Steven L. Blue

Imagine your company is a luxury ship navigating the choppy waters of the business world. At the helm of the ship is you, the CEO, sitting at the steering wheel, humming to yourself, all the while blissfully unaware of the mutiny forming below deck.

Just like the captain of the Titanic mistakenly ignored warnings of icebergs in the area, too many "captains" ignore the signs of toxic culture growing under their watch.

Endless, pointless meetings that eat up time and sabotage productivity.

Arbitrary promotions that destroy morale.

A revolving door of employees.

Recognition that's as rare as a purple unicorn.

All of these are bright red flags that if left unchecked will eventually sink your ship. And there will be no one to blame but you.

A healthy culture increases performance by five to ten times, yet most CEOs ignore it because they mistakenly think their job is to focus on strategy and data. Culture is relegated to a touchy feely "nice to have" afterthought.

But make no mistake, just because you haven't thought about culture doesn't mean you don't have one.

Culture exists. Period. If it doesn't exist by design, it exists by default. Every brand, every school, every church, every retail store has a culture, and that culture is either a powerful force for growth or an unrelenting force of destruction.

If you want to be a truly effective leader, you've got to realize that if you don't get culture right, you won't get anything right. It's the foundation on which everything else is built. After more than 40 years in leadership positions, I've developed a process that helps companies completely reinvent and shift their culture.

It's an in-depth process that asks you to rally your team to take three steps—transform, ignite, and disrupt!™

Consider this chapter your life preserver. I'm about to share with you an overview of the formula that has helped hundreds of companies revolutionize their culture and in turn, skyrocket their revenue and productivity. This process will help you build teams of top talent who are enrolled and engaged in your vision. It will position you as the best and most obvious solution in your market. And most importantly, it will prevent you from steering your ship right into the side of an iceberg.

THE PREREQUISITE

If you don't believe that culture can wreck your organization, I have two words for you. Wells Fargo. Wells Fargo has a culture grounded in what I call "bumper sticker" values. "Bumper sticker" values look good on paper but have no relationship to the real values of the organization. Their flagship bumper sticker values are "ethics", and "do what's right for the customer." Yet they employed deceptive sales practices and created over two million ghost accounts. Wells Fargo values profit above all else. The problem is the CEO was in fat, dumb, and happy land drinking the bumper sticker values Kool-Aid. By the time he realized the truth—that the company did not at all practice the values it preached—it was too late.

I cover a lot more of this in my book *Metamorphosis: From Rust Belt to High Tech in a 21st Century World*, but for now, what you need to know is that to truly transform your organization, you've got to begin with these three pillars:

Respect • Integrity • Teamwork

If you've ever caught a performance by the Blue Angels, you'll see these pillars in action. The Blue Angels are the Navy's flight demonstration team. Their mission is to showcase the excellence of the United States Navy and the team is held to impeccably high standards both in performance and conduct.

They rigorously train to fly all six planes as one cohesive unit which requires flawless synchronicity. After a demonstration, they gather to poke holes in their performance to continually strive for improvement.

From the top commander to the newest pilot, everyone is aware and on board with the team's commitment to their values. They've created a culture that enables the team to be high-performing and endlessly impressive.

What's happening within *your* team? Do you have bumper sticker values or real ones? There are a few things you can do to find out. First, do an organization-wide values check-up. But don't ask the executives. They'll tell you what you want to hear. Conduct anonymous surveys to find out what the real values are. You'll either be satisfied or terrified with the answers. If you're satisfied, great. If you're terrified, you need to do something about it—fast.

Next, determine a set of values that are meaningful to your employees. This is important. Concocting a bunch of values because you think they sound good isn't going to cut it.

Once you've got that dialed in, make sure the folks at the top believe the values, communicate them and demonstrate them every day.

Cultures are formed by values and organizational behavior. Wells Fargo engaged in deceptive sales practices because of sales compensation programs that incentivized them to behave that way. Be sure your policies support the new values and protect them vigilantly.

Don't let anyone in the front door that doesn't believe in them.

I don't care how good they are technically, if they don't believe in your values, don't hire them.

Yes, that means you might have to make some tough decisions and sacrifices, but guess what, that's what leaders do!

TRANSFORM

Many years ago I was negotiating a high-stakes agreement with a very hostile union. The stakes were so high that if I didn't get everything I needed to get, it would be the end of the company, thousands of people would be out of work and my career would likely be over.

We were down to the last two hours before the expiration of the agreement, and we were at a stalemate. The union walked into the factory and accused me of not negotiating in good faith. My choice was to walk away or lead the charge by making a demand of the union. To make a long story short, they offered to extend the agreement indefinitely. That wasn't going to work, so I delivered another risky ultimatum. I gave them one hour to deliberate. I told them if I was happy after that hour, I'd give them another hour and so forth. This was such a high-profile negotiation that TV cameras were parked outside, and my boss was calling every fifteen minutes for an update. In a final risky move, I shut off the phone and moved the negotiation to an undisclosed location. It worked, and we came to an agreement. Every decision I made during that experience could've gotten me fired, but instead, it solidified my reputation as a top negotiator.

Transforming your culture and your results starts with knowing where you are today, where you want to be tomorrow and taking educated risks to get there. You've also got to anticipate industry changes.

Thirty years ago, if you needed to research something, you picked up the Encyclopaedia Britannica. The encyclopedia was the mother of all resources for decades, but the rise of the digital age threatened its reign. After more than 240 years in print, Brittanica went digital and instead of seeing it as a defeat, the president of the company embraced it as an opportunity to become a dynamic and more up-to-date source of information.

Someone at Encyclopaedia Britannica should have talked to Kodak. Since the late nineteenth century, Kodak was the king of film photography. You'd snap a picture, send your film roll in for developing and a few days later, pick it up. The onset of digital photography made this long development process obsolete, but Kodak stubbornly believed no amount of innovation could dethrone them. They filed for bankruptcy in 2012.

If you want to transform your organization, you've got to be willing to take risks. Taking risks on a regular basis is the mark of a strong leader. Rookies wait to make hard calls until there's an emergency to react to. It's the equivalent of a hail Mary pass in a football game, which by the way are only successful 2.5 percent of the time.

Don't be a rookie. Go pro.

Ignite Innovative Thinking

Every organization can be innovative, yet most companies never tap into their full potential.

It starts at the top. The CEO must declare that it's time to innovate. Not HR. Not engineering. The CEO must stand strong and explain to the entire company that the doomsday clock is ticking.

This is particularly true in rust-belt, middle-market companies in so-called mature industries. The order of the day is disrupt or be disrupted, and you can't disrupt anything until you unleash innovational potential. A perfect example of this axiom is what happened to Blockbuster. Netflix innovated the model and disrupted it. Now, who is gunning to disrupt Netflix? Amazon, the ultimate disrupter. Disrupting the market requires innovative thinking and that's not a natural act. It's an intentional choice that acts as a catalyst to transformation and yet most companies don't do it. Why?

In my experience, it always boils down to one or more of four reasons.

1. Lack of belief—Most people don't believe they're inherently creative and therefore do not act accordingly. Hence, many companies don't believe they have the "right stuff" to innovate, and don't even try.

2. Lack of methodology—There is a methodology to ignite ideas and unleash creativity in any organization. However, many people believe creativity and innovation is a mystical beast that only appears in the minds of the Einsteins in the world.

3. Lack of resources—Some companies try to employ creative methodologies but don't provide the resources for them to take root. They don't view "this creative stuff" as the "real" work.

4. Lack of focus and commitment—Unleashing innovational potential takes laser-like focus and steely determination to see a project through, no matter what. Are you prepared to dismiss people if they won't go along with the innovational potential program? Are you prepared to go toe-to-toe with your board if they want to shut it down? Trust me, there will be plenty of naysayers all around. The best leaders cover their ears, ignore the noise and push forward.

Provide the time for people to brainstorm and unlock their innovational potential. At Miller Ingenuity, we allow for people to spend 20 percent of their time innovating. I even built an innovation space in our factory that the employees named "Creation Station." Innovative thinking requires space and time for the creative process. Yet, because CEOs can't *see* anything tangible happening, they dismiss it as unproductive and take it away, filling that time with soul-crushing meetings that serve no purpose.

Drive by a dairy farm. Are the cows standing there doing nothing? Or are the cows, in ways you cannot see from your car, producing the product that will make the money?

DISRUPT THE INDUSTRY

So you've set your goals and rallied your team to move toward transformation. You've got a killer set up that nurtures innovative thinking. Now you've got to disrupt the market.

Years ago the Department of State was running a tradeshow in a crummy space in Mexico City. Picture low ceilings and dark lighting in a dangerous part of town. A lot of people wanted to participate in the Mexican market, but no one was excited about getting on a plane to travel to what felt like a crime scene waiting to happen.

I wanted in. I asked the Department of State to partner with me so together we could move the venue and put on a better show. They declined. Undeterred, I found a great venue at a cool hotel in Monterey, a safe and beautiful town. I deployed a ton of marketing, which the Department of State arrogantly thought they didn't need to do and started a tradeshow business in Mexico. It was a big risk. I didn't know the Mexican market or the tradeshow business, but I knew *people*. I put up $100,000 as a personal guarantee to the hotel. The first issue was I didn't actually have $100,000 at the time. The second issue was an unprecedented snowstorm that hit the northeast of the United States, where most of my customers would be traveling from. I had planned for every possible contingency except mother nature.

Here's a tip for innovation and disruptive leadership—if what you're doing doesn't scare you to death, it's not worth your time.

It ended up being a huge success, but it was a success born from a willingness to take a chance and do things in a unique way. I see a lot of business leaders talk themselves out of things because "it's just not how it's done." To that I would say, "Exactly! All the more reason to do it!"

Another element to disruption is that you've got to make sure your brand is memorable, and sometimes the best way to do that is to loudly declare your differentiator even if it's not all that different.

Take Titos Vodka. Titos is known for being gluten-free but guess what? Most vodka is gluten-free. Titos was just the first to loudly declare it as a differentiator.

Gluten-free was a buzz phrase sweeping the nation and Tito's caught the wave. The key is to figure out a large, unmet customer need, find a position in the market where you can win, and tune into hot industry issues that haven't yet been claimed by another brand.

If you want to disrupt an industry and position yourself as the best and most obvious choice, be different. And if you can't be that different, be first and be loudest.

World's Largest Metaphor Hits Iceberg

That was the headline from the satirical newspaper *The Onion*, which called the Titanic a "representation of man's hubris."

The engineers of the Titanic thought it was unsinkable and that was an idiotic mistake. They didn't make enough lifeboats because who needs those on an unsinkable ship? Their arrogance sent them speeding through icy waters, ignoring all warnings. They botched and delayed evacuation because up until the ship snapped in two, they held onto their stubborn belief that other ships could sink but not *theirs*.

Most CEOs see culture as their company's version of an appendix. They know it's a thing, but they ignorantly believe that if they just focus on strategy, data and profit, they will be invincible.

"Great culture" is often thrown into a job posting as a fringe office perk, but the reality is that the right culture can produce higher revenue, unleash waves of new ideas and empower employees to go above and beyond the previous standard.

As Urban Meyer wrote, "Leaders create culture. Culture drives behavior. Behavior produces results."

Do whatever it takes to create a healthy culture. A culture by design, not by default.

Every day you have a choice in how you steer your ship. You can ignore what matters and repeat history's most disastrous headlines...or you can captain a vessel of innovation, strength and enduring success.

About Steven

Steven L. Blue is an internationally recognized expert on leading change and business transformation, showing companies how to triple and even quadruple growth.

Steve regularly contributes expert commentary and interviews with leading media and industry outlets, including FOX, *BusinessWeek*, *Forbes*, *Inc.*, *The Huffington Post*, *Entrepreneur Magazine*, *AMA*, *Europe Business Review*, *The Adam Carolla Show*, and *The Wall Street Journal*. His insights have led many media outlets to refer to him as one of America's leading mid-market CEOs.

Steve is the president and CEO of Miller Ingenuity, an innovative company revolutionizing traditional safety solutions for the rail industry. Its products protect assets, preserve the environment, and save lives.

As a best-selling author, Steve's five critically acclaimed books are written for executives, leaders, entrepreneurs, and anyone seeking to learn the secrets of success in the corporate world. He has earned the prestigious *Quilly*® Award and been inducted into The National Academy of Best-Selling Authors®.

Steve also joined with DNA Films®, an Emmy® Award–winning film production company, as a coproducer in a documentary chronicling the life and times of legendary marketing genius Jay Abraham.

Steve has served on a variety of boards in safety, banking, healthcare, and university business schools. He was named the first CEO-in-Residence for the College of Business at Winona State University. Steve was also invited to teach a leadership class to students at Vin University in Hanoi, Vietnam.

Steve holds a bachelor's degree from the State University of New York and an MBA from Regis University.

Connect with Steve:

- www.StevenLBlue.com
- Facebook: fb.me/StevenLBlue
- x.com/stevenlblue
- LinkedIn.com/in/stevenblue

CHAPTER 20

DRIVING EXCELLENCE

By Anjali Byce

In today's noisy, fast-paced, and sensory-driven world, silence can be extremely uncomfortable.

In fact, being quiet is a struggle for most humans, as we've grown accustomed to using background chatter, social media and other forms of noise to drown out the incessant hum of our own thoughts.

I know of people who challenge themselves with fitness goals, train for marathons, and push their bodies to the limit. But if you really want to find out how tough you are, go silent for ten days straight.

I signed up for a ten-day silent Vipassana retreat during college. Vipassana is one of the most ancient forms of meditation and one I yearned to experience myself. It wasn't easy for a chatterbox like me to go ten days without eye contact or conversation, but I was up for the challenge.

The first few days were the hardest. My thoughts raced, and the urge to talk was almost unbearable. I learned to observe my thoughts without judgment, letting them come and go like clouds drifting by. Slowly, I found a stillness I'd never known.

As I came out of the retreat, I wondered what my first words would be. It was like a hard reset of a computer! I lived with an intentionality I hadn't before, choosing every word carefully, weighing options to make decisions, and letting go of preconceived notions I'd been carrying.

Never did I imagine that the lessons I learned during those ten days would become my foundation for corporate leadership. It's natural to apply the qualities of clarity and mindfulness to a meditation retreat, but what I've learned is that those same qualities are the mark of successful leadership. Leaders must cultivate the ability to observe without judgment, listen intently, and understand the impermanence of both challenges and successes.

I would need these qualities as I embarked on my journey into adulthood. They would become my anchors as I navigated my career, stepped into executive positions, and ultimately forged my own path to abundance, excellence, and success.

BE BOLD; BE BRAVE; BE THE BEST; BE BYCE!

When I was in college, I was required to choose my major. In that era the popular choices were medicine and engineering, as those were "safe" occupations, but my heart was always drawn to psychology.

I was fascinated by people! I wanted to deeply understand why we behave the way we do, what drives us to succeed or causes us to fail. I've always been a quick study of other people. My father was in the Indian Navy, so we moved a lot, and I changed schools six times as a child. I learned early on how to navigate change and quickly connect to other people.

During each life change, I had an anchor to hold on to. It was the family motto our father instilled in us: "Be bold; be brave; be the best; be Byce!"

The spirit of that stays with me. It's a reminder to participate fully in life no matter where you are, to create your own space as a leader, and to always strive to be the best version of yourself.

Byce is our last name, and this motto reminds me that I'm born with everything I need to succeed. At the core of the motto is a commitment to excellence. It wasn't always easy, but I was determined to model it.

I remember as a student staying behind in India to study when my parents moved to Australia. My first time in a student hostel taught me valuable life lessons: the ability to stay anchored by my values, focused on my goals, and not swayed by peer pressure. I can see now how that molded me into the kind of leader who isn't afraid to make unpopular decisions for the good of the whole.

It also prevented me from being intimidated the first time I had to lead a team of people who were twice my age. Our motto to be bold allowed me to be myself. I didn't feel the need to act overly proper or professional or pretend to be more serious than I was. Being comfortable in your own skin is a driving force for success because when you're confident in who you are, you emanate an energy that other people can trust.

My father required us to play a team sport. There are few things in life that don't require interaction with and understanding of others. Teamwork teaches you how to listen, how to collaborate, and how to pick up the ball when it's dropped!

My mother embodied our family motto by working with people in need. Through her example I learned empathy and respect.

My work in human resources has allowed me to practice and live all these principles of success daily. A lot of people see HR as a job that's all about rules and paperwork but that's a narrow and misguided perspective.

The most important word in the job description is *human*.

I hear my father's voice reminding me to be brave, be bold, be the best, be Byce, and I am reminded that I am not just an HR director; I am a champion for human potential.

KNOW WHERE YOU'RE GOING, BUT BE PREPARED FOR DETOURS!

The road stretches out ahead of me, and I'm laser focused on tuning in to all my senses. My thoughts are a whirlwind of calculations. How fast can I take the turn without losing control? When should I accelerate? When should I slow down? I visualize the perfect ride, and my adrenaline kicks in as the roar of the engine vibrates with power.

I love driving, and in my spare time I love to travel and have even participated in a car rally. As we race, we've got to be cognizant of time, speed, and distance. All of it matters.

It has occurred to me over the years that the blend of focus and flexibility required for a successful race is the same blend required for excellence in business.

When you get behind the wheel of a car, you better know where you're going! Without a clear destination and a road map for getting there, you drive in circles or never leave the parking space.

And what happens if you take a wrong turn? Do you give up? Or do you recalculate and take an alternate route? How fast do you move toward your highest goals, and is there room for a change in direction?

My goal in both life and work is to drive excellence. You've got to start, however, with knowing what excellence means to *you*.

Once you can define success for yourself, the road to getting there becomes clear.

You've just got to keep your eyes ahead, your foot on the gas, and your focus on these mile markers of excellence.

THINK FORWARD

If you're embarking on a road trip, you need to have a destination in mind before you start your car. The same is true for life. I'm a big proponent of practicing the art of presence, but that doesn't mean we fail to look forward. After all, even if I'm driving to a beach destination, I am still fully rooted in the present moment, enjoying the feel of the road beneath my tires!

One of the best ways to practice forward thinking is to ask yourself this question: What do I want the headlines to say?

Whether we're talking about actual media headlines or not, it's a great metaphor. Imagine a newspaper is publishing an article about you and your greatest success. What does the headline say? What's the story about? What are the highlights printed in bold?

When you think of every goal as a potential front-page story, it helps you get granular about what you really want and the steps it will take to get there!

EMBRACE CHANGE

One of the marks of great leaders is their ability to stay agile and embrace change without sacrificing quality.

I have been in countless situations that required me to abandon plans I spent months creating. The market shifts, the team changes over, and suddenly all your best plans are irrelevant.

The staff looks to me, as a member of the executive team, for direction. That's a lot of responsibility! What if I take a wrong turn and the entire team follows me to a dead end? Whether you're leading a team or just trying to navigate life, you've got to remind yourself that every car can go in reverse, and you can make a U-turn at any time!

Life will change. It's inevitable. While you can't anticipate every change, you can choose to adapt to changes, recalculate the route, and keep moving forward with grace and confidence.

LISTEN

One of the benefits of a mindfulness practice like Vipassana is that it teaches you the art of listening. This would become a vitally important skill for me in high-stakes negotiations.

If while someone is talking, you're formulating a response in your head, you're not listening. You've tuned out half of what they're saying to focus on your own reply. You cannot drive excellence in work or relationships until you master the art of present and active listening.

This means fully engaging with the person you're speaking to without judgment or preconceived notions. It trains you to absorb not only their words but the nonverbal cues, such as body language, that give keen insight to what the other person truly wants.

As a result, you can navigate tough situations with ease and empathy. Whether you practice this in the boardroom or at home over dinner, it's the key to creating win-win scenarios.

SHARPEN THE AXE WITH CONTINUAL LEARNING

Most cars these days are automatic, but I love the thrill of driving a car with a manual transmission.

When you're driving a manual car, you must reduce your gear to gain power. This is a great lesson in cultivating elevated excellence. Most people think that the faster you achieve a goal, the better. They leave no room for slowing down, reassessing, and learning more.

Imagine a Formula One race car. How much detail do you think the driver can see at 230 miles per hour? It's all a blur! There's a time and place for speed, but sometimes you've got to slow down, look around, and learn new skills to meet changing tides.

Allowing room for continual learning ensures that you don't miss important details and that you regularly assess if your current path is the best one or if perhaps there's new information that could propel you forward.

Every organization goes through a time in which sales goals aren't met. And too often the solution is to work harder and faster to make up for lost time and revenue. Big mistake! What's the sense of moving faster in the wrong direction?

When I'm leading a team, my advice is always to take a step back. When we take time to study why the numbers aren't being hit and thoughtfully map out new protocols, we can move forward with confidence knowing we've addressed the root of the problems and won't likely encounter them again.

Like it or not, sometimes you've got to slow down to speed up.

GREET THE JOURNEY WITH A POSITIVE MINDSET

Back when I was in college, I studied very hard and was determined to find a good job. Any student who received an offer did not have to sit in on placement sessions, which were events students attended to meet hiring managers and find employment.

I received an offer from a great company, so I didn't attend the placement sessions. Then, quite unexpectedly, the company pulled all offers. For a moment I panicked! I had no job and had missed the opportunity to meet other companies.

Yet I was determined to stay positive.

One of the managers of the company that withdrew the offer was moving to a new organization and asked me to join him. It was a start-up, and I was employee number nine! I took a leap of faith, joined, and helped it grow, and now it's one of the largest conglomerates in the country!

I learned so much from that experience. As a member of the start-up team, you must be involved in every single decision. I was part of designing systems, processes, and procedures. I had to build the team, develop competencies, and manage the budget. It was tense, fast-paced, and a massive catalyst for growth.

It also taught me to lead with empathy, as I never wanted anyone to feel the panic I felt when my offer was pulled. At one point in my career, when one of our departments needed to close, I made sure 86 percent of the employees were placed in new positions. The others went out on their own. The entire process of building that start-up became an incredible foundation for me.

Imagine if I had stayed in despair and dismissed this opportunity!

Few of us can predict where life will take us, but if we're staring in the rearview mirror at the lost opportunity, we miss the new road in front of us. The most successful people I know greet every detour with a positive mind and total faith.

Staying positive isn't just a trend or a feel-good catchphrase. It's a powerful strategy for success.

AN ANCIENT TAKE ON MODERN SUCCESS

One of my favorite books is *The Bhagavad Gita*, an ancient Hindu text that holds great wisdom for a life well lived.

The *Gita* delves deep into the concept of dharma, which is centered around each of us living by a set of principles that guide us on our paths. The teachings encourage us to perform our duties with integrity and passion.

In a world in which success is often based on results, the *Gita* flips that paradigm and measures success by the way we conduct ourselves on the journey.

Do we act with diligence and integrity, or are we so attached to outcomes that we miss the lessons embedded in the milestones along the way?

Do we define success only as a target to hit or also as a way of being?

Are we measuring excellence by dollars and cents alone or by actions and character?

The Bhagavad Gita emphasizes the fulfillment of duties without attachment to results. In other words, focus on performing your responsibilities diligently, and success will be the natural outcome that will follow.

A skilled driver can simultaneously move forward, navigate obstacles, and enjoy the scenery, and we can do the same in life.

We can stay mindful but think ahead. We can drive forward but accept detours with grace and agility. And we can achieve our highest goals while still making time to listen, learn, and breathe.

In our lives and our careers, success is not just about reaching the destination; it's about the beauty of the journey itself, and the countless ways we can grow, connect, collaborate, and contribute along the way.

About Anjali

For over twenty-four years, Anjali Byce has built high-performing, agile, and culturally strong organizations. As chief human resources officer, she has spearheaded initiatives that foster high-performing teams and nurtured future talent. She places strong emphasis on culture, values, and diversity. Anjali's expertise spans across domains such as sales, strategic HR, organizational development, and more, embracing industries from engineering to insurance. Her capability to handle diverse business scenarios such as start-ups, corporate turnarounds, and acquisitions is evident during her association with global corporations such as STL, SKF, Thermax, Cummins, Allianz Bajaj, and Tata Motors.

A thought leader in the HR space, Anjali has enriched the industry with her insights, contributing to numerous publications and speaking at prestigious forums, including a panel discussion on "Women Leadership" at Harvard Business School. Her work has featured in various media platforms, including ETCIO, ETHRWorld, Outlook (India), BW-Businessworld, HR Magazine (UK), and The HR World, to name a few, demonstrating her influence in shaping HR practices globally.

Anjali's exceptional contributions have earned her significant honors, including being named CHRO of the Year 2020 by BW-Business World and securing a spot among the Top 20 Women HR leaders by People Matters. Her leadership and innovative HR strategies won her awards from CHRO Asia and World HRD Congress.

Beyond her professional achievements, Anjali is deeply involved in shaping the future of industrial relations through her active participation with the Confederation of Indian Industry (CII). She contributes to academic excellence as a corporate advisory board member with leading universities. Anjali is also a certified Marshall Goldsmith Stakeholder Centered Coach. Her continual learning journey includes certifications from revered institutions including MIT, Chartered Institute of Marketing (UK), and IMD (Lausanne), underpinned by a strong academic foundation in human resources from the Symbiosis Centre for Management. She is a Master in Applied Psychology from the University of Delhi.

Outside her professional realm, Anjali is passionate about mentoring young professionals and students, finding joy in hobbies such as driving, photography, and exploring culturally rich destinations.

Her foresight and ability to navigate ambiguity highlight her leadership in shaping thriving organizational cultures. Her impact extends beyond organizational success, shaping global HR practices with a focus on inclusive workplaces where every individual can thrive.

Her life's work stands not just as a testament to her prowess in the corporate world but also illuminates her commitment to making a positive impact on society and nurturing next-generation leaders.

Connect with Anjali:

LinkedIn: www.linkedin.com/in/anjalibyce

Website: www.anjalibyce.com

CHAPTER 21

A NEW DEFINITION OF SUCCESS

The Gateways to a Life Well Lived

By Cia Ricco

I was seventeen years old when my parents sent me to New York City with nothing but a few headshots and a suitcase.

My sisters both had special needs, and everyone saw me as the promising "normal" one. My parents were convinced I could make it as a model. I doubt they had any idea that plopping a small-town innocent girl into the underbelly of the modeling business would knock the "normal" right out of me.

My father took a few pictures of me, put me on a train, and told me to find a sponsor. I clutched my suitcase tighter as a man sat down next to me. He introduced himself and asked why I was going to New York. I had only one hundred dollars and noplace to go, so when he offered to help me, I accepted. Thus began a whirl-wind period of being passed from one photographer to another, most of whom required methods of payment having nothing to do with money. Soon, I was passed to some of the most notable names in the film and fashion industries. Oleg Cassini put me in his runway show and introduced me to some of the most famous people in the world. But it all came at a great cost. I was "given" to the famous movie producer Sam Spiegel and filmed a few parts in Rome. I spent months jet-setting with celebrities. I visited Monte Carlo, stayed in a castle on Lake Geneva, and luxuriated in the most glamorous hotels in Europe.

It was the most miserable period of my life.

The people around me were dripping in glitz and were the unhappiest, most unethical people I'd ever met. Looking out my hotel window at the stunning backdrop of St. Tropez, the disparity between the external beauty and my internal despair overwhelmed me.

I had to get out.

Finally, I met the then famous actor Lionel Stander. He somehow understood the emptiness in my eyes and gave me the money (and courage) to get out of Europe and back to New York.

I didn't have much to return to. I'd been betrayed by my modeling agency as they'd sold a nude picture of me to Playboy without my consent. Yet my tiny apartment felt like a haven compared to the debauchery I'd just been through. One day, while standing on a street corner, a young man approached and asked if we could talk.

We made our way to a diner, and he told me he was searching for enlightenment. Something in his words brought me to life and I felt a jolt of remembrance. This was why I was here—to find the light. I'd come into this world always knowing that my intention was to move toward enlightenment, but life had sidetracked me into a reality that was totally opposite of that.

He told me to go to a spiritual bookstore and trust my instincts. I chose two books, one by Krishnamurti and one called *The Secret of the Andes*. The latter described a mystical place in the Andes mountains where enlightened elders lived.

I was about to make the first of many decisions led by my intuition and embark on what would become a lifelong quest to deeply know myself.

A Girl, a Donkey, and a Life-Changing Journey

After meeting my "guru" in the diner, I felt an urgent need to shake off the debauchery of my modeling and acting days. I had a plane ticket credit that was about to expire. With my book on the Andes in hand, I decided to fly to Bolivia, get a horse, and ride over the mountains. Perhaps enlightenment lived in the Andes.

With nothing but a backpack, I landed in Bolivia and learned that my desire to find a horse was naïve. There were none! I bought a donkey instead. I loaded my few possessions on my donkey and walked with her over the mountains. It was a remarkable spiritual journey not because it led to enlightenment but because it didn't.

I no longer believe there is such a thing as *finding* enlightenment. I've discovered that it's not a place to get to or search for. Enlightenment is present and alive in every moment if we are. In those mountains, in total solitude, I practiced the teachings of Krishnamurti based on the art of awareness. I had nothing else to do. Imagine going from the sensory overload of New York to total isolation, with nothing but a donkey and the stars to talk to!

I practiced so deeply that even in sleep I was in meditation.

The contrast I felt once I was back in New York was extreme. I felt lost. I had to earn a living and eventually became a call girl. This was surprisingly liberating because, for the first time, I set the terms. I worked in "the oldest profession" for two years, using the money to put myself through massage school. I kept my massage work strictly legitimate but felt like I was straddling two worlds. As the journey through the Andes became a distant memory, I temporarily stopped searching for any kind of answer.

They say when we give up searching, the guru appears. And that's what happened.

I was living above the Mercer Arts Center on Broadway. There was a large space that was used to play public access videos. One day, I heard the voice of a guru and the words sounded like a truth I'd been longing for.

The man playing the video invited me to visit the guru, Trungpa Rinpoche, in Colorado. I went and Trungpa came onto me. It wasn't for me. My friend took me to a more traditional Tibetan Buddhist teacher who became my teacher for twenty years. Yet it wasn't enough. I could meditate so well I could get my teeth drilled without flinching, but my life still didn't work!

One day in a doctor's office, I saw a catalog for Opening the Heart workshops. My twenty years of studying Buddhism allowed me to recognize resonance when it came my way. Before I picked up the catalog, I knew I'd go. And that it would change my life.

The Gateways to Success, and to Life

The workshop didn't allow distractions. There were no clocks, TVs, or telephones. It was disorienting, but soon I knew this was the work I wanted to do for the rest of my life.

Back then, you didn't need a license to practice therapy in New York, and even as the laws changed, I was grandfathered in as a psychotherapist.

Through this work, I came to recognize that I'd been living in shame and hiding. I understood, finally, the importance of self-love in truly becoming whole. I knew I couldn't help others until I was whole myself. My discoveries during this period are reflected in my first book, *Living as if Your Life Depended on It: Twelve Gateways for a Life That Works*. The Gateways that came through became the roadmap for my life and I've lived them ever since, as well as using them to help thousands of others heal their lives.

Here are a few you can turn to when you need a north star, a gentle nudge or road map back to your own heart.

Stand in Your Truth

Moving into alignment with our values shakes things up big time. Working in the sex industry was easy, guaranteed money, but it wasn't aligned with who I was. I felt like I had a split personality. It was then that I grasped the true meaning of integrity, which means "wholeness" or "completeness." We are neither whole nor complete unless we're living by our values.

As I reflected on the deep sense of fragmentation I'd experienced throughout life, and the pain of betrayal in my early years, I recognized a vital missing ingredient: truth. I vowed never to lie to myself or another ever again.

It wasn't easy. When you commit to living in alignment with

yourself, you'll upset people, as you'll disrupt an equilibrium they've grown accustomed to. And that's fantastic. Because the more willing you are to upset the balance of what *isn't* true for you, the closer you come to What *Is*.

Learn to Love Yourself

There is no other more powerful gateway to a life well lived than learning to love and trust yourself. It's the key to joy. I had to accept, forgive, and love myself unconditionally before I knew what happiness was.

Your most extraordinary life is so close. The deepest love, the most fulfilling experiences, and the manifestation of your wildest dreams are waiting for you. Until you are willing to love yourself unconditionally, drop all the negative self-talk that stands in your way, and accept the wholeness that is you, you will not find peace, joy, or genuine love.

All you need to do to claim your true birthright is hold your head high, trust the guidance of your own inner voice, and boldly step through the gateway to meet your true essence and calling.

Accept What Is

Years of living in toxic environments eventually took a toll and I became ill. I developed an auto-immune disease, low blood sugar, chronic fatigue, fibromyalgia, serious allergies, and a general relapsing-remitting illness that I live with to this day.

I consider my illness one of my teachers in living the Gateway of Accepting What Is.

One of the biggest barriers to happiness is resisting what's in front of us. We resist the diagnosis, the end of a relationship, a change in jobs. All our misery and exhaustion comes from our tendency to battle with what happens, instead of accepting it as the next benchmark on our journey.

When you learn to surrender to what's coming *now*, you open your energy to what's coming for you *next*. As you learn to trust that it's not a punishment, but a beautiful unfolding, you'll sink into a deeper level of contentment.

For me, illness liberated me from fear. A stubborn resolve took root and I refused to let any of it stop me from pursuing my dreams.

I would live, thrive, and lean fully into the next gateway.

Harness the Power of Choice

All through life our inner knowing drops hints in the form of dreams, goals, and moments that awaken dormant desires.

Harnessing the power of choice is the act of courageously following our intuitive nudges even when it doesn't make sense!

Twenty-three years ago, I left the country. I wanted to be somewhere remote and peaceful.

I sold everything and moved to Costa Rica, sight unseen. I picked the spot intuitively by putting my finger on the map. Sure enough, it was perfect, a two-hundred-acre ranch on a mountain overlooking the gulf. Like a scene from a movie, I negotiated the deal on horseback from the mountaintop and moved into a tiny shack with one rusty pipe for water, one light bulb and a wood-burning oven. I built the shack into a house and sold it for enough money to construct a retreat center. I pursued my charity work for teens in need there and met a boy living in deplorable conditions whose mother had just died. I took him in and began the long several-year saga of trying to adopt him.

I decided while in Costa Rica to live every one of my dreams. As a child, my fantasy was to have a herd of horses. I rescued, birthed, and trained horses in Costa Rica until I had a herd of twenty-four. I loved sailing, even though I knew nothing about it, so I bought an old wooden sailboat and learned to sail. I always wanted a hot-air balloon, so I trained, got a pilot's license, bought a balloon, and had it shipped to Costa Rica. I enjoyed an amazing life in Costa Rica for seventeen years.

Sixteen years later, I developed cancer and moved to Sarasota, Florida for treatment. I am still there and, at the time of this writing, six years cancer-free. It was a great test of my "Let Go" Gateway, where I write about the acceptance of death and living as if "today is a good day to die." I call this phase of my life my bonus round. I live every day in awe and gratitude as if it were simultaneously my first and my last.

Only *you* can decide what this one wild and precious life will look like. There is no limit to how much joy you can feel or how many dreams you can chase if you just allow yourself to harness the power of choice!

Develop a Tolerance for Joy

It's a funny way to word it, right? Why would we need to learn to *tolerate* joy? The reality is, as much as we say we want to be happy, it's harder for us to experience joy than any other emotion. Why? Think about how many times you were joyful as a child and told to "settle down!" We learn that being joyful is selfish or unsafe. Or we attach our joy to transient things like jobs or relationships and become undone when that source of joy is gone.

The key is to find joy in things that cannot be taken from you. Maybe you learn to feel joy in the simplest moments, like the first sip of coffee each morning or the colors of spring. Maybe you spend time serving others. Allow yourself joy with no guilt or fear. We weren't put on this earth to suffer, despite what it might feel like sometimes. We're all born with the capacity to choose, to change, to rise.

Be Willing to Change

You have everything you need. Now take the leap!

With no degree other than a license to practice massage, I became a therapist, a teacher, an author, a retreat leader, a horse ranch owner, a minister, a pilot, and many other things that on paper I'm not "qualified" for!

I've never let that stop me.

If you look at the definition of the word "life" it is this: the condition that distinguishes animals and plants from inorganic matter, including the capacity for growth, activity, and continual change preceding death.

Growth, activity, continual change.

That's life!

The true qualifications come from a willingness to seize opportunities with courage and an open heart. You have everything you need within you to pursue your dreams.

True success is in reaching a place of balance, self-awareness and joy, a state of mind that can only be reached through a willingness to be fully alive in every moment. A successful life for me is about feeling whole and complete.

All it takes is the commitment to loving and knowing yourself, the willingness to follow your own intuition, and the courage to step boldly through the gateways as the audacious spirit you are into the adventure that awaits you called *life*!

About Cia

Based on her own life experiences and Buddhist background, Cia Ricco has honed her craft for over thirty-five years as a psychotherapist, coach, teacher and author.

Having been abused as a teen and young adult, she now helps teens and young adults. She founded Visions and Dreams for Creative Learning, Inc., a 501(c)(3) to help youth in need. Being self-taught, Cia now trains therapists in body-centered work.

Cia built and ran a retreat center in Costa Rica for over fifteen years where she adopted a teenage boy and founded a micro-lending bank to help local women. There she continued conducting programs for at-risk and disenfranchised youth while running healing retreats for adults and commuting to the US to teach workshops.

Currently living in Sarasota, Florida, Cia works with individuals, couples, and families via Zoom. She also runs private in-person healing and recovery retreats and psychotherapeutic intensives out of her home, as well as leading group retreats and trainings nationally and internationally. Her current passion is a series of Deep Dive Psychotherapeutic Retreats featuring optional psychedelic-assisted therapy series to increase depth of perception, heal from trauma, overcome fear of death, and deepen your connection with All That Is.

Ricco's books and audio books include *Living As If Your Life Depended On It, From Self-Worth to Net Worth, Inner Seasons, Learning to Love Yourself,* and *Manifesting Abundance.*

Cia was a frequent teacher at centers such as Kripalu Center for Yoga and Health, Omega, the NY Open Center, Wainwright House, and many others. Her workshops have included "Create the Life You Want," "Love Sex and Soul," "Discovering the Goddess Within," "Deep Peace," "Living Ageing, and Dying," "Trainings in Body-Centered Psychotherapy," and others that she is delighted to custom-design. She is a professional speaker, had a radio program, and has been a guest on radio shows and podcasts.

Cia's methodology is unique and based upon the Twelve Gateways she has developed and outlined in her first two books. A student, practitioner and teacher of Buddhist and other meditation and healing techniques for over fifty years, Cia brings a sense of safety, serenity, and spirit to her life and work. She is passionate about helping others to heal from trauma and teaching them in turn to access their own inner guidance that they, too, may live a more integrated, authentic, conscious and joyful life at any age.

Learn more at www.CiaRicco.com.

CHAPTER 22

IN THE EYE OF THE STORM

By Devi Jade

It's the sounds I'll never forget.

The most intense test of my life came when I was in a horrendous car accident during a routine trip to the post office.

That's usually when life's most jarring moments happen, when we're not anticipating them in the least. In a flash the chatter of my babies and the music from the radio was replaced with screeching tires, metal crashing against metal in bone-rattling impact, glass shattering, and then…silence.

The car spun in what felt like slow motion, and we careened off the road, landing in a bog. My heart pounded, and my hands desperately searched for my children as the pungent smell of water and soil seeped through the broken windows.

And that's when I looked up and had a vision. I saw Jackson, my ten-month-old baby, in heaven. He was smiling and waving at me.

"*No! Come back,*" I pleaded with him, "*Come back.*"

But he kept waving, and I kept begging, until the vision closed. I turned to the back seat and saw the gray color of death on his face.

I woke up in the hospital, and as my eyes adjusted to the harsh lights, my mind immediately went to my children. By the grace of God, they revived Jackson. Jackson, Bryce, and my unborn baby all survived the horrific crash. But my marriage would not.

I lay on a gurney in the dark hallway for hours. No one came to check on me. No one came to listen for my baby's heartbeat. That night after hours had passed, my husband finally came to see me but had no words of comfort or love.

I knew in my heart that it was over and that this day would mark the start of a whole new life.

It had to.

How Will You Live?

I had always been a gifted child. From the time I was a baby I had gifts of clairvoyance and clairsentience. I could actually see my ancestors, angels and even Lord Jesus. My childhood was wrought with abuse and neglect, and I believe that my connection to God and my ability to transcend this earthly plane is the only reason I survived.

I continued to have visions, and when I told my family, they would say it was my imagination. After an abusive foster mother discovered my gifts and did her best to beat them out of me, I learned to temper them and fall in line as best I could. Later I received the Holy White fire, the power of the Holy Spirit, and joined the LDS church. Little did I know it was also a church that prized patriarchal roles and the subservience of women. I did what I was told, honored the church's directive to procreate, and participated in all the required ceremonies.

After my first child was born, my marriage began to fall apart. I did everything I could to connect to my husband. When he took up bodybuilding, I did too! I went on to win multiple competitions, but that seemed to only anger him further and his cruelty deepened. Each time I'd try to leave, I'd be reminded by him and the church authorities I needed to keep the commandments, so back to him I would go.

I could feel my spirit begin to fracture, but guilt is a strong foe, and despite my intuition desperately trying to remind me of my own power, I continued to have his children and pray for a miracle.

But that day in the hospital, when he had no words to comfort me, it became clear. This wasn't love, and I would not continue to subject my children or myself to this abuse. What happened next is something I can only describe as the hand of God reaching down and touching my head. My body may have been broken, but I felt my spirit come to life. I was filled with the kind of conviction that can only come from the Holy Spirit. I knew when I got out of that hospital, I would be a different woman.

I would open my heart back up to the gifts God had given me and I would, at last, step into my divine destiny!

What Are You Devoted To?

It didn't happen overnight. Like most lifelong programming, it takes time to break free. I didn't leave immediately and went on to give birth to our son Lawson. One day, though, not long after he was born, I was hunkered down in fear beside my dresser, terrified of the chaos unfolding between me and my husband. Suddenly, a small voice from within said to me, "If you stay, this is how you will live the rest of your life. This is what your children will model."

Enough was enough!

Once I was on my own with the children, a whole new world opened and the gifts I had hidden for years returned stronger than ever. I was consecrated to the Hindus, the Lakota Sioux, the Buddhists, the Christians, Mother Mary, Saint Joseph and Lord Jesus, and Celtic traditions. I understood many religions and spoke to all the deities. These were my gifts.

It became crystal clear what my spirit needed more than anything was devotion to the mission that was placed inside me.

Think of a challenge you've faced—a toxic relationship, an illness, a decision—and ask yourself this question: At that time, what was I devoted to?

I realized during my marriage I was devoted to being the obedient wife, without ever stopping to consider the cost, without ever stopping to truly ask God if it was worthy of my devotion.

I see people all the time who are devoted to the very things they long to get away from. They are more devoted to their illness than to health, talking incessantly about their symptoms instead of picturing themselves well.

I see people more devoted to their image than their truth. What about you?

Are you devoted to the problem or the solution?

Are you devoted to the expectations of others or to the dreams God has whispered to you?

The word *devotion* is defined as love, loyalty, and worship. Are the things you're giving your time, energy, and heart to *worthy* of love and loyalty?

That day in the hospital, I knew what I was devoted to. I was devoted to Lord Jesus, my children, and the gifts bestowed upon me as a vehicle for helping others in need.

I had been broken in every way a human can be broken. I was deeply intimate with pain and because of that, I could see it in others. I could speak to it, heal it and release it from their lives.

My devotion is to my beloveds; it knows no bounds, and I will fiercely protect it, because when we devote ourselves to the light, the light devotes itself to us.

What Do You Hold Sacred?

After my divorce a friend suggested I go to an Inipi ceremony or sweat lodge ceremony.

I immediately said no, having no idea what it was, but he assured me I could leave if I felt uncomfortable. The experience was life-changing. I felt I was a part of Mother Earth, a part of the whole, that heaven and earth came to the center of me. It was an experience I will never forget.

I realized a practice or ritual doesn't become sacred because an authority figure deems it so. Things become sacred when your experience of them moves you closer to a higher power. Over the years, I became a Grand Master Sacred Heart Fire Energy healer, a Wisdom Keeper and Medicine Woman for the Lakota Sioux tribe, a mentor and teacher, all in the name of living my sacred purpose to heal "All Our Relations."

You have a sacred purpose too. It lives in the quietness of your spirit and waits patiently while you take every path but the one that opens its door.

We live in a fast-paced world. Our minds are overloaded, and our definitions of love and success are warped by the media and society. We strive and hustle when our bodies are begging for rest. We continue to suffer even when it insults our souls. We do this because we've lost touch with our sense of the sacred.

It's so easy to get wrapped up in busyness that we fail to hear the messages from within. This is how we end up trapped in love-less relationships, passionless jobs, and everyday realities that exhaust us and dilute our gifts.

When your heart is hurting, when you feel disconnected, ask yourself this: What do I hold sacred?

What are you doing when you feel closest to God? Where are you when you can feel the frequency of the universe coursing through your veins?

And how can you bring more peace into your life?

One of the fastest ways to restore sacred ground within yourself is to remember that you were born divine!

You are a divine creator. At any moment, you can take a breath, leave the story you're in, and choose a new one. You can decide to rewrite your story, knowing that whatever you do will guide you to your true mission, leading to your highest good.

You are *always* empowered to change, to leave, to grow, to fight, to heal, to *win*. You were born with the ability to regenerate your body, mind, and spirit, but life caused temporary amnesia!

It's time to return, to restore, and to remember your power.

What Do You Seek?

I trained for years to become a Medicine Woman for the Lakota Sioux tribe. The Lakota are deeply spiritual people who honor their connection to the divine through traditional sacred rites. One of those rites is the Vision Quest.

The purpose of a vision quest is to pray and attempt to receive messages imparting deeper understandings of life. To receive their vision, the person commits to staying in an isolated place in nature for one to four days with no food or water.

At the heart of this journey is solitude.

Not many people make time to sit in solitude and commit to sitting until holy guidance comes through. It's in the silent moments you hear the whispers from Spirit and receive your vision and mission.

In my fourth and final year of Vision Quest, I visited the elders. A sacred fire was being prepared and would be lit soon after I was prepared for my quest. All on its own, the fire started and grew to eight feet high! The elders had never seen that happen, so it was then that I was asked to carry the sacred peace pipe, which holds a direct line to the Creator. This was very rare, as often only men were asked to carry the pipe, which signified carrying the wisdom for all Sioux people, and I was deeply honored. During my vision quest I took the pipe and sat so long on the hill that the tribe's holy man had to come and retrieve me. I was determined to stay until an answer came through. (Sometimes the lack of a vision manifesting is the answer that's meant to be interpreted.) As I sat there, a male moose walked right up to me! Moose symbolizes sacred "knowing." I knew it was time for me to lead and heal.

What I know now is the most revered holy people on earth saw visions and were courageous enough to share them.

Every single one of us receives divine guidance and intervention; we're just programmed to dismiss it. How many times have you seen something and thought, "Maybe it's a sign," before dismissing its potential wisdom and going on with your life? Or perhaps you saw something out of the corner of your eye and convinced yourself it was nothing.

Or maybe you needed guidance, came across an animal, and

didn't think twice about why a bird, an insect, or a tree was put in your path.

We are trained to dismiss divine messages even though we are constantly, consciously and subconsciously, seeking them!

All our lives we wrestle with decisions yet ignore the wealth of guidance readily available to us all. We hold tight to control, reluctant to surrender or acknowledge our humble place in the world. Yet it's in surrender we find exactly what we're looking for. You don't have to be a religious person to experience this kind of sacred connection and communication. You simply have to create the conditions for insights to emerge.

The vision quest is not just a traditional rite of passage for the Lakota Sioux but a transformational experience for anyone seeking spiritual guidance in life. The wisdom of the quest invites you to look within, connect with the natural world, and trust in the guidance that emerges from your deepest self.

Who Will You Be?

To me the greatest definition of success is a life lived in harmony with your true nature. And in our true nature we are deeply connected to our Creator, to one another, to Mother Earth, and to all universal wisdom.

For decades I hid my gifts. Since returning to my true nature, my entire life has changed. I have been honored to heal thousands of people, taken part in thousands of sacred ceremonies, and dedicated my entire life to helping others find their true paths.

My divine connection was always there. I simply needed to decide to live it out in the open, no matter what.

To decide is our greatest power. We come to this earth as a seed, and as we grow, it doesn't matter if we grow into a tiny flower or a giant redwood. What matters is that you *decide* to grow, that you take your place in this world as the divine being you are.

No matter where life takes you, returning to these questions will walk you home.

What are you devoted to?

What do you hold sacred?

What do you really seek?

Who will you be, how will you live, and what will you give?

My journey was not easy. I was beaten, broken, and betrayed. Yet the significance of those experiences pales in comparison to the beauty of my redemption, the strength of my conviction, and the unbreakable bond that exists between me, the divine, and *you*!

Remember, at any moment, success in life rests in your innate faith, deciding to take action, and knowing that you *will* succeed. When night falls, the sun still shines; we just can't see it. The same is true for life! The light is always there.

If you can't seem to see it, *be* it.

Sometimes when you can't *find* the answer, you *are* the answer.

About Devi

Devi Jade is a revered mystic and seer. A mystic is born with sacred gifts of knowledge, direct communication with the divine, and initiation into sacred mysteries by higher beings. A seer predicts or foresees future events and conveys their messages. Together they serve humanity and all that encompasses our world.

With over thirty-five years of dedication to spiritual service, Devi Jade's influence reaches the world through divine teachings. She shares wisdom and sacred guidance, inspiring thousands on their spiritual journeys. Devoted to Lord Jesus, Mother Mary, the Holy White Fire (the power of the Holy Spirit), holy angels, and saints, Devi Jade guides individuals according to their Akashic records, bringing healing and inner peace.

Devi Jade embodies the divine feminine and is the keeper of wisdom and holy woman of the Lakota Sioux. She receives direct guidance for your healing and well-being. She received the Holy White Fire from Blessed Mother Mary to assist in deep body healing. As a grand master of Sacred Heart Fire Energy Reiki, she teaches and initiates students worldwide. Consecrated to Lord Yeshua, Mother Mary, initiate of His Holiness the Dalai Lama, and Babaji, Devi Jade integrates all practices for healing.

Devi Jade is a master trainer in NLP since 2008, a certified trainer for trainers under Jack Canfield, and a graduate of Tony Robbins trainings. Renowned globally for her specialization in spirit, mind, body, and soul purpose, she leads spiritual and educational courses.

As the founder of Cisnebella Inc. in 1994 and Bella Warriors Retreats, Devi offers exclusive retreats for healing and deep inner transformation. She recently established The Sacred Heart Fire Energy Reiki Mystery School, dedicated to sacred healings for humanity, animals, and the earth.

Her commitment to the global community focuses on spiritual awakening. As an advocate for interconnectedness and unity, she promotes the philosophy that "We are all related," engaging in communal service to promote world healing and preservation.

Devi's influence extends beyond her teachings and retreats. She offers her books on wellness, poetry, and children's books. Her life and work are a testament to her profound devotion to holy deities, fostering spiritual awakening, and promoting holistic growth and unity.

Learn more:

- www.cisnebella.com
- www.bellawarriors.com

Follow Devi Jade on social media:

- **Facebook:** Devi Jade Moser
- **Business Facebook:** Cisnebella, Bella Warriors
- **Instagram:** @Cisnebella
- **LinkedIn:** Devi Jade
- **YouTube:** Devi Jade

CHAPTER 23

THE ART OF LISTENING AS A BRIDGE TO CONNECTION AND SUCCESS

By Rita Montgomery

"Wisdom is the reward you get from a lifetime of listening when you'd have preferred to talk."
—DOUG LARSON

I had spent weeks meticulously planning every detail of my three-year-old daughter's surprise party.

The house was decorated with colorful balloons and streamers, and our friends and family were all gathered, excited to give this party for our sweet girl. We huddled in the dimly lit room, whispering and giggling, as we awaited her arrival, imagining her little face lighting up with joy.

Finally, the moment arrived. The front door creaked open, and as she stepped into the room, we jumped out and yelled, "Surprise!"

But instead of the joy I had envisioned, her eyes went wide with terror. She froze, and then let out a heart-wrenching scream, bolting out of the room with tears streaming down her face.

The room fell silent, and my heart sank. I rushed after her and tried to calm her down and get her to rejoin the party. Her reaction was a huge shock to me, but three-year-olds are nothing if not unpredictable, so I tried to put it out of my mind. Yet something in my gut was telling me this was more than a tantrum.

She was born a healthy child, but when she was about a year and a half old, I noticed a few things. She didn't seem to be making eye contact, and when she would walk or run, she did so with her head down. She had some speech issues, but when I would express concern, friends, family, and even doctors would reassure me that all kids develop at different rates. Soon, though, she no longer wanted to be held or hugged, and something as simple as a tag on the back of a shirt could send her spiraling. When other kids were around, she would play near them but never with them.

She was an only child, so I wondered if these were behavior issues, the product of getting all the attention. Then I chalked it up to the fact that she was probably just a tenacious and strong-willed child, marching to the beat of her own drum. But as the situation got worse, my frustration grew, and I wondered if I had done something wrong.

Was it my parenting? Was it something I ate during the pregnancy?

We had her tested for Asperger's when she was seven, and though the test came back negative, her struggles intensified. One thing was clear: My gut instincts were right. My child, like 15 to 20 percent of the population, was displaying neurodivergent traits, and not enough people understood what that meant or how to help.

Neurodiversity describes the idea that people experience and interact with the world around them in many different ways. Those who understand neurodiversity see these differences as a fact of life rather than a deficit.

The reality, however, is that most people *don't* understand it, and I would watch my daughter struggle through life with no idea how to help her. It's heartbreaking to watch your child suffer and to be unable to offer comfort or solutions. Then one day not long ago, my daughter, who is now thirty years old, sat down with me and explained the lens through which she saw the world.

It turns out if I wanted answers on how to help my daughter, all I needed to do was ask her, and most importantly, *listen*.

I realized after that eye-opening conversation with her that I had read and studied and made medical appointments, but what

I hadn't yet done was master the art of listening. Most of us listen like we are scanning headlines, pulling out the words and phrases we *think* are important and mentally preparing our reply.

The true art of listening, however, isn't about your ears hearing the words that are said but rather your mind and heart understanding the words that *aren't* said.

Whether you have a neurodivergent person in your life or not (and you may and just not know it), the art of listening will not only deepen your connection to other people but massively increase your chances of successful communication, foster an environment of mutual respect, and, above all, pave a path to peace.

Here's how to do it.

TRUST YOUR INSTINCTS

My intuition started speaking to me very early on in my daughter's life, but everyone from school officials to doctors and even my own family told me it was nothing. Back then it wasn't as big of a conversation as it is now, so a lot of kids with autism went undiagnosed and didn't receive the help they needed. Trust your instincts! If something feels off, it probably is. This is true in any conversation you might be having with a friend, family member, or colleague at work.

Pay attention to the nonverbal cues of the person you're talking to. Do you get a feeling that they are shrinking back? Do they seem uncomfortable? Is the energy between you open and clean or full of tension?

Your sixth sense should never be discounted, and this is especially true in your relationships. How many times has a relationship or situation gone south, and you've said to yourself, "I had a feeling that was going to happen!"

Those aren't just feelings; they are clues, like breadcrumbs, leading you to the truth.

OPEN YOUR MIND

Open Google and type "career advice" in the search bar.

You're going to get thousands of results that offer well-meaning advice on how to nail a job interview, how to be assertive, or how to have a difficult conversation with your boss. The problem is that all those search results are written for neurotypical people.

When my daughter was twenty-eight, she finally sat down with me and described the world through her eyes. She shared that she had spent her life trying to please others and be accepted, and it didn't seem like anyone else was attempting to understand or accept her in return. She struggled to adapt to a world that seemed to have no intention of returning the favor.

When she entered the workforce, the typical advice put the pressure on her to adapt and conform to the "normal" expectations of communication, which was often harmful, exhausting, and counterproductive to everyone involved.

She felt that she was set up for failure, as her natural way of being was automatically considered a deficit. That's why part of the art of listening is keeping an open mind and remembering that there is more than one way of experiencing the world.

The French language is no better or worse than the English language; they are just different. The same is true for neurodivergent and neurotypical people and all humans in general.

We all communicate differently. Our inflection and tones may differ. Our body language may differ. Yet our intentions and goals may align. That's why it's vital that we stay open to the fact that while someone may communicate differently, what they have to say is valid.

Shift your focus from their delivery to their words and most importantly to their intentions.

CHECK ASSUMPTIONS AT THE DOOR

When my daughter was in school, she was very isolated. She had few friends, as people often misunderstood her behavior. She didn't make eye contact, but that didn't mean she wasn't listening. Still, that trait fell outside the "norm" and people assumed she was being rude and disrespectful.

Everyone processes the world differently. Some people are very literal, and sarcasm is lost on them. Others interrupt, not because they don't value your words but because their brains are working at lightning speed.

One of the things I learned to do with my daughter, which translated into how I learned to listen to everyone in my life, is focus on the result of the conversation, not the physical delivery. Did we achieve our goal? Was it peaceful? Did both sides participate? If the end result was a mutual understanding, it didn't matter much if she was looking at me, the floor, or the ceiling!

I also learned not to assume meaning. When someone shares something with me, I attempt to paraphrase it back to them to ensure that my own biases haven't colored my understanding. I wish I had known that when Jennifer was younger. As parents we have a bad habit of assuming we know what our child is trying to say instead of respecting them enough to ask for clarification.

We come by our assumptions honestly. They are formed from our own experiences, our childhood programming, our fears and expectations. Releasing those assumptions is a vital element of the art of listening, no matter who you're talking to.

With our guesses out of the way, we are one step closer to connection, empathy, and truth.

MASTER SILENCE AND CURIOSITY

Epictetus said we were given two ears and one mouth so we could listen twice as much as we speak, yet we all tend to interrupt.

Whether you're trying to calm a child or lead a meeting across a negotiation table, the less you say, the more you'll learn. It's not easy. Sometimes our brains are working fast, and we fear that if we don't express a thought, we may lose it. Yet talking over people or finishing their sentences rarely leads to mutual understanding and often results in the other person feeling bulldozed and disrespected. Now remember, a neurodivergent person may do this without realizing it, but if you are doing it as a neurotypical person, it's a habit you can and should change!

One of the challenges Jennifer shared with me is that most people are watching the clock and fail to give enough time and grace for communication to take place. If she's struggling to find words, the silence becomes uncomfortable and the person she is talking to will remedy that by speaking *for* her. Then, to avoid confrontation, Jennifer goes quiet and lets them take over, which results in them missing out on the benefit of her often brilliant perspective.

This is a problem in relationships too. We all come to relationships carrying the wounds and programming of our childhood. Your naturally loud voice could feel threatening to someone who grew up in a household wrought with chaos. My tendency to talk fast, born from never getting a word in edgewise as a child, could feel frustrating and overwhelming to a partner who takes time to process things. That's why we've got to get curious.

One of the things I have learned to do with Jennifer and with anyone I'm speaking with is ask about their preferred method of communication. I get curious about what medium they prefer, if they prefer literal communication or can tolerate some sarcasm without getting offended, or if they seem to respond better to a quiet or commanding voice.

You can go by trial and error, but if time is tight, and if the relationship matters to you, simply ask.

IF I KNEW THEN WHAT I KNOW NOW...

Like most parents, there are a lot of things I wish I could go back and do differently. If I knew then what I know now, I would have treated Jennifer's behavior not as a problem to be cured but as a new language to learn or a puzzle to solve.

I would have fretted less and listened more. I would have labeled her differences not as deficits but as diverse perspectives that could massively expand and broaden my own understanding of the world.

About a year and a half ago, she participated in a work project, and the program director understood autism and gladly adapted the project to suit her. It was a huge success. She is articulate, independent, and highly intelligent. My hope is that the world will not miss out on all that's beautiful about her while looking at only what's different.

If I had embraced her unique way of experiencing the world earlier, I could have become her strongest advocate much sooner. The more I learned to truly listen and understand her, the more I realized how much she had to teach me. Listening isn't just about hearing words; it's about understanding the meaning behind them and recognizing the value in different ways of thinking and being.

Jennifer's journey has taught me that when we take the time to truly listen, to get curious, to open our minds and hearts to new perspectives, we open ourselves up to a richer, more colorful, and more inclusive world.

About Rita

For over forty years, Rita Montgomery has been a lifelong learner—with her greatest and wisest teacher being her daughter, Jennifer. Passionate about the art of communication and offering guidance and support for parents of neurodiversity children, she speaks from her own life and experiences.

As a college instructor, communication skills were part of the curriculum she taught. Jennifer's journey showed her that when we take the time to truly listen, to get curious, to open our minds and hearts to new perspectives, we open ourselves up to a richer, more colorful, and more inclusive world—a valuable lesson she instilled in others.

Rita received her university education in Saskatchewan and British Columbia. The next years were spent living in Western Canada, as her career and personal life took her to explore the beauty of Canada.

Her newest venture is to coauthor this book, *Unlocking Success*, with Jack Canfield.

Rita also enjoys time spent traveling to visit family, engaging in conversations with new people, and enrolling in new courses to expand her mind. Currently, Rita resides on beautiful Vancouver Island, British Columbia—close to her daughter and two rambunctious boys, her cats named Valki and Kytheon.

For more information or to inquire about booking Rita for a presentation, please visit www.ritamontgomery.com.

Email her at qofg2117@gmail.com.